D

HOPE THIS BOOK
GIVES YOU MANY
HAPPY HOURS ENCOURAGE
MENT FOR YOUR
GARDEN.

WITH LOVE
THE UGNE EMMUS!

# Keith Kirsten's Gardening Solutions

# Keith Kirsten's Gardening Solutions

Human & Rousseau
Cape Town    Pretoria    Johannesburg

With thanks and appreciation to the publishers, to all who allowed us
to photograph their gardens, and to the following people
for their co-operation and contribution: Fillis Meyer, Gerald Schofield,
Stuart Barnhoorn, Allison Brett, Margie Foggitt and, last but not least, to
Lizelle Meyer-Faedda without whom this book would not have been possible.
Thank you so much!

**Front cover:** *Rosa* 'Raubritter'

**Photographic credits**
Jerry Harpur: front cover and pp. 8; 11; 13; 18; 20; 34; 39; 48; 51; 54; 72; 78; 83; 85; 94;
    104; 109; 115; 116; 118; 121; 123; 131
Nancy Gardiner: pp. 26; 28; 30; 32; 33; 53; 57; 62; 75; 82; 86; 91; 100; 103; 136; 150; 153; 156
Keith Kirsten: pp. 42; 47; 58; 64; 66; 69; 71; 76; 101; 111; 113; 120; 126; 128; 132
At Schoeman: pp. 134; 139; 140; 142; 147; 148
Dimitri Nenkov: pp. 15; 40; 96; 99
Raymond Hudson: pp. 74; 106; 114
Brian Krull: p. 93

Copyright © 2001 by Keith Kirsten
First published in 2001 by Human & Rousseau (Pty) Ltd,
28 Wale Street, Cape Town
Typography by Etienne van Duyker
Cover design by Chérie Collins
Line drawings by Moira van Winkel
Text electronically prepared and typeset in 9.5 on 12 pt Avante Garde
by ALINEA STUDIO, Cape Town
Colour separations by Virtual Colour, Paarl
Printed in China through Colorcraft Ltd. Hong Kong

ISBN 0 7981 4136 0

# contents

# introduction

Planting and maintaining a garden is instantly gratifying and brings years of pleasure and reward. Whether we live in a city, a rural village or on a farm in the country, we feel compelled to plant a garden, be it formal or informal, trees and woodlands, vegetables, herbs, fruit trees, or water gardens designed to suit our needs.

Over the years, gardening styles have undergone marked changes, mainly owing to a greater awareness of design and gardens becoming smaller. Modern garden practices, advanced machinery and equipment and better services have also changed gardening methods. Plant varieties have similarly not remained static, with new plants continually being found in nature or being especially cultivated.

As a result of smaller living spaces, there is today greater emphasis on instant and more mature specimen plants, on colour, containers and plants suitable for these. Also popular are herbs, vegetables and fruit (or small kitchen gardens known as potagers), and attracting wildlife to the garden with indigenous plants and other accessories.

The eradication of alien species or plants classified as harmful weeds is high on the agenda of environmentalists and gardeners alike. These unwanted aliens impede the growth of our wild vegetation, impact negatively on agricultural crops, reduce water tables and limit the aesthetic potential of our country.

In your pursuit of the ideal garden, you are bound to come across the same old problems and difficulties which have troubled gardeners over the centuries. This book will assist you to overcome many of them. The chapters are divided into various gardening categories, which will help you find the solution to your particular problem as quickly as possible.

Since indigenous plants are gaining in popularity and are playing an increasingly important role in our gardening activities, I have highlighted these with an asterisk* throughout the book, that you may gain maximum benefit from our impressive flora.

Happy gardening!

KEITH KIRSTEN
27 October 2000

This magnificent avenue of camphor trees (Cinnamomum camphora) at Kirstenbosch was planted around 1898 by Cecil John Rhodes in honour of Queen Victoria.

# landscaping

A beautiful garden grows from good planning and design and should reflect the taste and preference of its owners. In South Africa, with its warm climate, most gardens have become an extension of the home and can be used for outdoor living, entertaining and recreation.

These days most gardens are enclosed spaces and people are striving to bring nature back into their gardens, as so much of it is rapidly disappearing. People are fortunately coming to appreciate the great value of indigenous plants, as water-wise gardening is becoming increasingly important. Indigenous plants also have the added benefit of attracting birds and butterflies to the garden. A good selection of indigenous and exotic plants suited to the climate of the region together with good design will make a successful garden.

## Planning and design

Planning and design are very important when you start a new garden or remake an old, overgrown or neglected garden. Your age and lifestyle, personal preferences and requirements will determine the style of your garden.

If you have a very busy lifestyle and lack the necessary time or money to maintain a garden, you may have to consider a low-maintenance garden, for instance one with a formal design or a design with little lawn and lots of paving and permanent plants. If, on the other hand, you have children and pets you will need lots of open space with lawn. But whatever your garden's function, you should make sure that its design reflects your own style and that of your house, be it formal or informal.

## Garden styles

Formal gardens are usually small to medium-sized and laid out on a level or terraced piece of ground. They can be either classic or modern in style, with symmetrical and geometric shapes.

Informal gardens are usually large to medium-sized and situated on a slope or uneven terrain. They can have many different styles, for example tropical, cottage, Japanese, Mediterranean, indigenous, etc.

Depending on its size, a single garden can have more than one theme. By dividing the garden into different areas one can have, for instance, a gravel garden, a children's play garden, a herb garden, a meditation garden, a shade garden, a woodland garden, an Italianate garden, a Japanese garden, a rose garden, a vegetable garden, a barbecue or patio area, etc.

It is a good idea to keep a scrapbook of different gardens that have caught your fancy, to help you decide on a style and theme for your own.

An informal planting gives a natural look to the borders. Note the open, uncluttered lawn.

## Limiting factors

First take stock of your garden or proposed garden and take a realistic look at limiting factors in order to determine your priorities.

■ The climate will determine the types of plants you use in your garden. It is no use trying to grow tropical plants from the coast in dry inland regions that suffer from cold and frost during winter.

■ The type of soil plays an important role. Different soil types influence drainage, soil condition and the pH of the soil. These are all factors that will need to be taken into account. If the soil is heavy and does not drain well, underground drainage will have to be installed or sand will have to be mixed into the soil, depending on the situation.

■ Where possible, try to retain existing plants, such as mature trees and shrubs, and remove only those that do not fit into the overall plan or theme.

■ Neighbours and existing features such as walls, trees and noise may be limiting factors. Unsightly walls and noise will need screening, while large neighbouring trees might pose competition for your garden. Suitable plants will have to be chosen to cope with the situation, or paving can be considered.

■ Services like underground cables and water pipes must be taken into account. Do not plant large plants over water pipes or cables, as pipes might be damaged by aggressive root systems.

■ Municipal regulations such as covenants and regulations on heights, types of walls and other structures may all influence the final design.

## General principles

Garden design is not achieved by following rigid rules and regulations, but should be inspired by one's individual taste, imagination and artistic sense. There are, however, general principles one should follow to create a successful garden.

**Unity:** The garden should be a reflection of the style and architecture of the house, with different parts of the garden blending into a pleasing whole.

**Harmony and contrast:** Lines, forms and shapes should flow together harmoniously to enhance the style of the house. Contrast is achieved by combining straight lines with curving shapes and by using different foliage textures and colours. Colour can also be used effectively to create an impression of depth in the garden, for example by using bright colours in the foreground and soft muted colours in the background.

**Proportion and scale:** This is the relationship between the different dimensions. Use features, plants and elements in scale with the house and surroundings.

**Balance:** This is the careful distribution of features without necessarily spacing them equally far apart. A well-balanced garden gives a feeling of stability and restfulness.

**Focal point:** This may be, for example, a pond or water feature, or a group of striking plants that focuses attention and adds interest to the garden.

**Creating vistas:** The illusion of distance and space can be created or a view can be framed by either trees or a Moon Gate or arch. These tend to concentrate the observer's attention, rather than allowing an all-encompassing view of the garden.

The gazebo used as a focal point at the end of a pathway through a rose garden accentuates the formal design of this garden. This is a good example of proportion and scale.

## A practical start

Tackling the garden in a haphazard way without prior planning can cause great confusion. The best way to go about designing a garden is to do it on paper. A garden plan is essential to help carry out one's intentions and as an aid in estimating quantities if the garden is to be planted in stages. It is also much easier to make changes or rearrangements on paper than in the garden itself.

*Drawing up a plan*

1.  On a sheet of graph paper, make a drawing to scale of the house and the boundaries of the plot. Write down all the information gathered at the site, such as existing features and structures like entrances, trees, paving, water pipes, neighbouring buildings or trees that will shade different areas, and note the points of the compass as well. This scale drawing will serve as the basis for designing the garden.
2.  Lay a sheet of tracing paper over the scale drawing and mark the various areas such as the entrance area, the lawn area, the children's play area, the patio, the paved area, etc. Remember not to have too many areas in a small garden as it will look and feel very busy. You can play around with these areas until a pleasing effect is achieved.
3.  Once these areas have been designated, lay another sheet of tracing paper over the first and draw in the lines of beds, pathways, paving, features like pots, garden furniture, etc. Here you can once again play around with different shapes and sizes until a balanced and satisfactory design is achieved.
4.  Only now may the placing of plants begin. Try to visualise the chosen plants in three dimensions and place trees and larger plants first, followed by smaller shrubs and perennials and, finally, by ground covers and annuals. It is always a good idea to visit a reputable nursery or garden centre with trained staff to help with the correct choice of plants.

You are now ready to start your garden. If cost is a factor, you can always apply the final touches to the various areas in stages. It is important, however, to plant large trees first as they will be permanent features and serve as a framework for the garden.

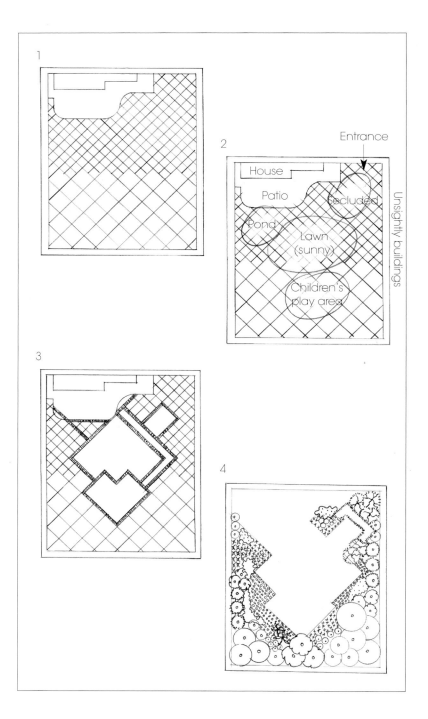

A garden sculpture surrounded by lush plants always adds interest to a garden.

# Questions and answers

**Q: We have just bought a large suburban house with a badly neglected and overgrown garden. What is the best way to plan a renovation without making mistakes?**

A: Depending on the amount of money you want to spend, you can either consult a landscape architect or go about rejuvenating your garden yourself. Do not be overhasty – take time to assess the good and the bad points first. Many shrubs may only require good pruning and feeding to come into their own. Start with the worst feature and assess its worth; eliminating the worst situations will enable you to start planning with what is left. It will also be easier to choose the type of garden you want. An area with lots of trees, for example, can be converted into a woodland garden. Areas where the lawn does not grow because of too much shade or too-heavy traffic can be converted into a gravel garden, or the area can be paved, planted with a shade-loving ground cover or mulched. There is a wide range of materials available to choose from. Another alternative would be to remove lower branches from trees to let in more light for the plants and lawn under them to grow again. It is very important to draw all existing features to scale on graph paper, as explained under the heading "Drawing up a plan' on page 12. Then take your plan to a reputable nursery or garden centre and get expert advice on plants to choose for the different areas, if you haven't been able to make a choice yourself.

**Q: I have a small townhouse garden. Which design would suit it best: a formal or informal one?**

A: The architecture, shape and topography of the area will determine the design. A level area with a geometric shape would be ideal for a formal garden, whereas a sloping and irregular shape would be better suited to an informal design.

**Q: We have bought a piece of land on which to build a house. Is there anything we can do before building starts to improve the site and save time later on?**

A: By conferring with the building contractor you will be able to determine where existing trees and shrubs should be retained. Remove all unwanted plants. It is not a good idea to start planting trees before building starts as they may be damaged or destroyed during building operations.

**Q: Can you suggest some shrubs and perennials for planting in the shade? We experience some frost in winter.**

A: *Acanthus mollis* (wild rhubarb), *Acer palmatum* (Japanese maple), *Ajuga reptans* 'Catlin's Giant' (large-leafed carpet bugle), *Alocasia* spp. (elephant's ear), *Asparagus* spp., *Aucuba japonica* (Japanese laurel), azaleas, *Camellia japonica*, *Clivia* spp., *Coprosma repens* (mirror plant), *Cyathea* spp. (tree ferns), *Cyrtomium falcatum* (holly fern), *Dicksonia antarctica* (Tasmanian tree fern), *Fatsia japonica* (Japanese fatsia), fuchsias, *Hydrangea macrophylla*, *Mackaya bella* (forest bell bush), *Mahonia lomariifolia* (Chinese holly grape), *Nandina domestica* (sacred bamboo), *Ochna serrulata* (plane bush), *Philodendron selloum*, *Phormium tenax* 'Pink Stripe' (pink-striped flax), *Pieris japonica* (lily-of-the-valley bush), *Plectranthus* spp., *Rumohra adiantiformis* (seven-week fern), *Sarcococca confusa* (Christmas box), *Zantedeschia* spp. (arum lilies).

**Q: Could you list some smaller trees and shrubs that would be ideal for a townhouse garden?**

A: Please consult your local nurseryman on the hardiness and suitability of the following plants for your area.
**Trees:** *Acacia pendula* (weeping myall), *Acer buergeranum* (small Chinese maple), *Acer palmatum* (Japanese maple), *Brachylaena discolor* (coast silver oak), *Buddleja saligna* (false olive), *Calpurnia aurea*

A problem area where the lawn didn't grow well because of too much shade was successfully converted into a focal point by mulching and a bench.

(wild laburnum), *Cornus florida* (flowering dogwood), \**Cussonia paniculata* (mountain cabbage tree), *Dais cotinifolia* (pompon tree), \**Diospyros whyteana* (bladdernut), \**Dombeya rotundifolia* (wild pear), \**Halleria lucida* (tree fuchsia), *Heteropyxis natalensis* (lavender tree), \**Loxostylis alata* (tarwood), *Morus alba* 'Pendula' (weeping mulberry), \**Noltea africana* (soap dogwood), \**Podocarpus elongatus* 'Blue Chips' (yellowwood), \**Rhamnus prinoides* (dogwood), \**Rhus chirindensis* (redcurrant), *Salix caprea* (goat willow), \**Schotia afra* (Karoo boer bean).

**Shrubs:** \**Acmadenia heterophylla* (buchu), \**Agathosma ovata* 'Kluitjieskraal' (false buchu), *Azalea* 'Christmas Cheer' (dwarf red azalea), *Azalea* 'Violacea Multiflora' (small violet-purple azalea), *Berberis* 'Red Jewel' and 'Rose Glow', *Berberis thunbergii* 'Atropurpurea Nana', *Callistemon citrinus* 'Little John' (miniature bottlebrush), *Coprosma* 'Rainbow Surprise', *Cotoneaster apiculatus*, *Cuphea hyssopifolia* (false heather), *Cuphea ignea* (cigarette bush), *Duranta* 'Sheena's Gold', *Gardenia augusta* 'Radicans', *Grevillea* hybrid 'Mount Tamboritha', *Hebe* varieties, *Helichrysum italicum* (curry bush), \**Hemizygia obermeyerae* (pink mist bush), *Hydrangea macrophylla* 'Winning Edge', *Hypericum x moserianum* 'Tricolor', lavenders, *Leptospermum* 'Cherry Brandy' and 'Nanum Kiwi' (miniature tea bush), *Melaleuca bracteata* 'Golden Gem', *Myrtus communis* 'Compacta' (dwarf English myrtle), *Nandina domestica* 'Pygmaea' (dwarf sacred bamboo), *Nerium oleander* 'Dwarf Salmoni', \**Polygala fruticosa* 'Petite Butterfly', *Punica granatum* var. Nana (dwarf pomegranate), *Rosmarinus officinalis* 'McConnell's Blue' and 'Prostratus' (rosemary), *Sarcococca confusa* (Christmas box), *Serissa foetida*, *Syzygium paniculatum* 'Globulum' (dwarf eugenia), \**Thamnochortus cinereus* (silver reed), *Trachelospermum jasminoides* 'Chameleon' (variegated star jasmine) and all the smaller conifer varieties.

**Q: I would like a statue in my garden. Can you advise me on how to place it?**

A: In small gardens one must be careful not to overdo the use of statuary. One good piece, not too big, would be sufficient as a focal point. A statue is usually placed at the end of a vista or in front of a background of evergreen shrubs. It needs a green background to fit into the garden. Avoid the use of brightly painted figures like gnomes, ducks, toadstools, etc.

**Q: Could you advise me on the best way to place a birdbath and what type to choose?**

A: Birdbaths should be placed in a sheltered spot surrounded by plants to give the birds some protection and a place to perch. There are many types of containers available, with and without pedestals, and made of concrete, clay, terracotta, metal, stone or fibre cement. Select an unobtrusive design which suits the style of your garden.

## Q: What is topiary work?

A: It is the pruning and trimming of hedges, shrubs or trees into specific shapes, such as geometric forms, figures, animals, etc., and is generally used in formal gardens with a Victorian theme.

## Q: What is an espalier and which plants can be used to make one?

A: It is a plant that has been trained through special pruning to grow flat, generally in a fan shape, against a wall or fence. It is an excellent way of utilising small spaces and making dull walls look more interesting. Ideal plants for espaliering are deciduous fruit trees, crab apples, *Camellia sasanqua*, magnolias, jasmine and honeysuckle varieties, *Cotoneaster horizontalis*, mock orange, dogwood (*Rhamnus prinoides*), flowering quince.

## Q: Which trees can be planted as screens and windbreaks and for what distance will the windbreak remain effective?

A: A windbreak is usually effective for about 20 times its height. Ideal plants for screening and windbreaks would be *Arbutus unedo* (strawberry tree), *Buddleja saligna* (false olive), *Brachylaena discolor* (coast silver oak), *Callistemon citrinus* (lemon bottlebrush), *Ceratonia siliqua* (carob), *Cryptomeria japonica* (Japanese cedar), *Cupressocyparis leylandii* and *C. leylandii* 'Castlewellan Gold' (Leyland cypress), *Cupressus torulosa* 'Compacta', *Dovyalis caffra* (Kei apple), *Lagunaria patersonii* (pyramid tree), *Ligustrum ovalifolium* 'Aureum' (California privet), *Melaleuca bracteata*, *Olea europaea* subsp. *africana* (wild olive), *Pittosporum eugenioides* (tarata lemonwood), *Pittosporum tenuifolium* varieties, *Pittosporum viridiflorum* (cheesewood), *Podocarpus* spp. (yellowwoods), *Prunus laurocerasus* (English laurel), *Photinia x fraseri* 'Red Robin', *Quercus ilex* (holly oak), *Rhus lancea* (karree), *Rhus pendulina* (white karree), *Salix mucronata* (safsaf willow), *Syzygium paniculatum* (Australian brush cherry), *Tecomaria capensis* (Cape honeysuckle), *Xylosma senticosa*.

## Q: We would like to have a swimming pool put in. What are the things to keep in mind when planning for a pool?

A: The shape, size and situation are very important. Keep the style of your house and garden in mind when choosing the shape and size. The pool should be placed close to the patio of the house to become an exten-

sion of the entertainment area, in full sun and sheltered from wind. Or if the garden is large, the pool can be placed at the bottom end of the garden with a large open lawn in front of the pool to provide an interesting focal point. Pools should not be placed in the middle of the garden, as fencing and planting around the pool will break up the garden. Remember also to make provision for camouflaging the filtering equipment and leave enough space for a paved area around the pool. Avoid deciduous and berry-bearing plants close to the pool. Certain evergreen and flowering plants like Australian bottlebrushes continually make a mess in a swimming pool.

**Q: Could you list some weekend projects to improve an old, established garden?**
A: You can build a herb garden with a sundial, or put in a bog garden, or renovate an old fishpond, restore paving and paths or lay flagstones in areas where the lawn does not want to grow, plant colourful annuals in containers, put up nesting logs and birdfeeders, put up trelliswork against an unsightly wall and plant a creeper against it, make a meditation area in your garden, make a gravel garden, a Japanese garden or plant some plants that would attract birds and butterflies.

**Q: Where should pathways be located and what material should be used for them?**
A: Pathways are important in a functional way and can have a profound influence on the garden. A badly made or placed pathway can destroy the outlook of an otherwise good-looking garden. A pathway breaks up the area and should not be used in small informal gardens. Pathways in formal and geometric gardens are usually part of the design and are not necessarily functional. Pathways in both formal and informal designs are generally used to draw attention to a feature like a garden bench, a birdbath, a statue or a pond, etc. Never put in a pathway if it does not lead to a specific destination. Materials suitable for pathways are bricks, slate, tiles, pavers, stepping stones, gravel and sleepers. Concrete and tar are very hard-looking and are not suitable for use in home gardens. One can lay bricks in many different ways, and slate, tiles and pavers can also be used to form a solid path. Alternatively, the openings between the slate, tiles or pavers can be planted over with grass or a suitable ground cover. Be careful, however, not to choose tiles with a too-smooth surface as these become very slippery when wet. Gravel pathways are very effective in informal gardens with an indigenous theme. Remember always to choose pathway material that suits the style and architecture of the house.

**Q: I want to make a scented garden. Please list some shrubs with scented flowers or aromatic foliage.**
A: **Shrubs with fragrant flowers:** *Abelia* varieties, *Buddleja* varieties (butterfly bush and sagewood), *Brunfelsia* (yesterday, today and tomorrow), *Choisya ternata* (Mexican orange), calamondin, *Cytisus praecox* 'Albus' (bridal broom), *Duvernoia adhatodoides* (pistol bush), *Euryops virgineus* (river resin bush), *Gardenia* varieties, *Heliotropium arborescens*, *Jasminum humile* 'Revolutum' (yellow bush jasmine), *Lonicera nitida* (box honeysuckle), *Murraya paniculata* (orange jessamine), *Osmanthus fragrans*, *Philadelphus coronarius* (mock orange), *Pittosporum eugenioides* (tarata lemonwood), *Plumeria* spp. (frangipani), roses (English roses), *Xylotheca kraussiana* (African dog rose).
**Shrubs with aromatic foliage:** *Acmadenia heterophylla* (buchu), *Aloysia triphylla* (lemon verbena), *Helichrysum italicum* and *Hypericum revolutum* (curry bush), lavenders, *Leptospermum liversidgei* 'Mozzie Blocker', *Myrtus communis* (myrtle), rosemary, *Salvia africana-lutea* (beach salvia), *Tarchonanthus camphoratus* (wild camphor bush).

Topiary trees, paving and a sundial give structure to this formal Victorian garden.

# soils and fertilisers

Knowledge of your soil and how plants grow in it is the most important aspect of gardening, as it will help you to water and fertilise your garden correctly. Plants are factories, which take raw materials from the soil, air and water to manufacture carbohydrates, proteins and fats. For this process a constant supply of energy, which is provided by sunlight and raw materials, is necessary. Chlorophyll, the green pigment in plants, carries out photosynthesis by absorbing energy from sunlight and using it to convert carbon dioxide from the air and water from the soil to carbohydrates and oxygen. Fertilisers are necessary because soils may not always consistently supply all the nutrients a plant needs to manufacture essential carbohydrates. Without an adequate supply of nutrients plant growth is poor and slow, which makes the plant susceptible to diseases and attack by insects.

Plants depend on soil for water, nutrients and support by roots that anchor the plant. The root system absorbs water and dissolved nutrients from the soil through the root hairs and passes them to the other parts of the plant. Roots need air to be able to perform their task of absorbing and conducting.

Soil is composed of mineral particles, living and dead organic matter, water and air. The size, chemical composition and form of mineral particles determine the structure of the soil. Sand particles are the largest, break down slowly and have large spaces between them. They hold water and nutrients badly and drain very fast. They have good aeration and are easy to cultivate. Clay soils are composed of microscopically small mineral particles which are tightly packed together, making for poor drainage and aeration. Clay soils retain plant nutrients well and are difficult to cultivate. Loam soils are those in-between soils with a mineral composition of clay, sand and silt particles. Loam is the ideal soil because it drains well without drying out quickly and contains enough air for healthy root growth.

## Organic matter

Organic matter is the decaying remains of once-living plants and animals and the droppings from birds and animals. It also includes earthworms, insects and micro-organisms such as bacteria and fungi which are the important agents in creating fertile soil. Gardeners add organic matter to improve and maintain the soil's texture and to encourage healthy root development; in other words, it acts as a soil conditioner. Organic matter will improve aeration and drainage of clay soils and in sandy soils will help to hold water and dissolved nutrients better.

Organic soil amendments cannot be overemphasised. These include compost, manure, leaf mould, peat moss, sawdust, bark, etc. Micro-organisms in soil that break down organic matter are directly responsible for the production of nitrogen, phosphate and compounds of potassium, calcium and other elements essential for healthy plant growth. The micro-organisms that do this need nitrogen, water, air and warmth themselves. Any organic matter that is added to the soil will thus improve the efficiency of soil organisms at their job of making nitrogen available. Organic materials alone, however, cannot supply sufficient plant nutrients and chemical fertilisers are essential to supplement the nutrient value of the soil.

Common sense suggests that the ideal situation would be to use both organic matter and chemical fertilisers for optimum results.

An example of a healthy and well-fed cottage garden.

# Inorganic soil amendments

These are useful as a supplement to organic matter. They are used to improve the texture of clay soils and may help sandy soils by increasing their capacity to hold water and nutrients. Vermiculite and perlite are examples of inorganic soil amendments and are used on a small scale in potting soils and small beds to help with water- and nutrient-holding capacities.

Lime and gypsum are used to improve clay soils by causing the particles to group together into larger units, which will improve aeration and drainage. The pH of the soil determines the use of gypsum or lime. For acid soils, usually in high-rainfall areas, lime is used and for neutral and alkaline soils, usually in low-rainfall areas, gypsum is applied.

Lime alters the soil pH and is a supplier of calcium. Gypsum is a supplier of both calcium and sulphur.

## Soil pH and lime

It cannot be taken for granted that all essential elements present in a soil will automatically be available to plants. The availability of essential elements depends on the acidity or alkalinity (amount of lime) in the soil. Soil acidity or alkalinity is measured on a scale of pH units, which range from 0,0 (the most acid) to 14,0 (the most alkaline) with 7,0 being neutral.

In very acid soils (pH 4,0 to 5,0) all the important elements are not readily available. In soils with a pH level of 7,5 and higher, phosphorus and other elements become unavailable. Most garden plants grow well in a soil with a pH of 6,0 to 7,0 as all elements are readily available in soils with this pH range.

The pH of soil can be checked with pH-testing kits available from most leading nurseries.

## How to raise pH

Agricultural lime or dolomite (calcium carbonate) is the best to use in this case. It does not react with other fertilisers if applied at the same time. Slaked lime (calcium hydroxide) can also be used but reacts with some fertilisers, resulting in bad side effects.

## How to lower pH

The best way to acidify alkaline soil is to use sulphur (flowers of sulphur). Sulphates can also be used in the form of iron sulphate or aluminium sulphate (alum). Organic material like peat moss, leaf mould, pine needles and well-composted sawdust will also lower pH.

# The basic nutrients

## Macronutrients

The three major macronutrients essential for all plant growth are nitrogen (N), phosphorus (P) and potassium (K).

*Nitrogen* is necessary to maintain healthy green leaf growth, as it is a vital part of chlorophyll (the green pigment in plants). Nitrogen-deficiency symptoms are stunted growth with pale green and yellow leaves.

Nitrogen fertilisers vary in the amount of nitrogen available to plants. Ammonium sulphate, urea and limestone ammonium nitrate (LAN) are available fertilisers containing nitrogen. It leaches quickly from soil and needs to be applied at regular intervals. Nitrogen also causes chemical burn if care is not taken to water adequately after application.

Fertiliser which contains nitrogen in slow-release form prevents damage from chemical burn. Slow-release nitrogen has made it possible to fertilise your garden with more user-friendly fertilisers like SR 3:2:1 (28) for lawns and the general fertilising of shrubs, trees and climbers, SR 3:1:5 (26) for roses, fruit, flowers and vegetables, Wonder Nitroacta Chip for lawns, Grostix Foliage 5:1:5 (22) for all pot plants and Supra 4:1:1 (18) plant food sticks for beautiful ferns and palms, to name some available ones.

The SR fertilisers have distinct advantages over ordinary granular fertilisers in that:

- Fewer applications per season are necessary because of higher nitrogen content and low-leaching properties, with no risk of burning.
- Nitrogen is released by biological action, providing the nutrient in a highly acceptable form as and when the plant needs it.

*Phosphorus* is essential for cell development and promotes good root growth.

Phosphorus-deficiency symptoms are poor root development and stunted growth, sometimes coupled with purplish discoloration of leaves.

Superphosphate is a fertiliser containing only phosphorus. However, there are fertiliser mixtures available that contain phosphorus. This nutrient does not leach very easily and for this reason must be applied to the root zone of plants when trees and shrubs are planted.

*Potassium* promotes chlorophyll formation, plays an important part in the strength of cells and encourages flower and fruit formation. Potassium-deficiency symptoms are weak stems, while older leaves may be floppy and have yellow or brown tips or margins. Potassium is needed in small amounts at regular intervals and is included in fertiliser mixtures.

Fertiliser mixtures consist of combinations of nitrogen, phosphorus and potassium in different ratios and are identified by N:P:K. A fertiliser described as 2:3:2 (22) contains two parts N (nitrogen), three parts P (phosphorus) and two parts K (potassium) in 22% available plant food.

## Secondary macronutrients

These are calcium (Ca), magnesium (Mg) and sulphur (S) and occur naturally in most soils.

*Calcium* is important in the construction of cell walls and promotes proper functioning of growing tissue. It is rarely deficient, except in extremely acid soils.

*Magnesium* is a part of chlorophyll and is thus important in photosynthesis. Magnesium deficiency can be seen in yellowing leaves, especially older leaves, but rarely occurs as magnesium is adequately present in most soils.

*Sulphur* forms a part of plant proteins and is involved in the formation of chlorophyll. Sulphur deficiency shows up as stunted growth and yellow foliage, similar to nitrogen deficiency. It is very rare, as most fertiliser mixtures contain sulphur.

## Micronutrients

Micronutrients or trace elements are necessary in very small quantities. These are iron (Fe), zinc (Zn), manganese (Mn), boron (B), molybdenum (Mo) and copper (Cu). Deficiency of micronutrients is extremely rare. They are included in plant food formulations like Nitrosol, Seagro and Kelpak.

## Fertiliser types

Organic fertilisers include manure, compost and green manure crops. See pages 27-29.

Inorganic fertilisers are made up with differing formulations for a variety of specified uses. There are granular and powder types in bags and boxes and liquid formulations in bottles, which can all be very confusing if not understood.

- Complete fertilisers contain all three major macronutrients, N:P:K, which are depicted as 2:3:2 (22) or 2:3:4 (21). They are generally applied at a rate of 60 g/m$^2$ or four tablespoons/m$^2$.

- Special-purpose fertilisers are specially formulated for certain plants, for example Blue Hydrangea Food, and straight fertilisers are made up out of an individual plant nutrient like LAN.
- Liquid fertilisers come in a variety of formulations and include organic fertilisers, complete fertilisers and special-purpose fertilisers, for example Nitrosol, Supranure Plus and African Violet Food.
- Slow-release fertilisers, such as 3:1:5 (26) SR, are specially made to release their nitrogen at a steady rate.
- Fertilisers with insecticides such as Wonder 4:1:1 (21) + Karbaspray are prepared in combination with an insecticide.

Most fertilisers give recommended amounts and application rates on their labels. As a general rule one should always start to feed plants when the new growth season starts in spring and then repeat at four- to six-week intervals until autumn at label-recommended rates. At the same time, remember to keep plants well mulched at all times.

## Questions and answers

**Q: I have been told to use Epsom salt in the garden. Why, where and how should this be used?**
A: Epsom salt is magnesium sulphate. Magnesium (Mg) is an essential part of chlorophyll and is therefore important in photosynthesis. Lack of magnesium causes yellowing of leaves, especially older leaves. Dolomitic limestone is a source of magnesium but does not produce satisfactory results because the magnesium is released very slowly. Epsom salt is much easier to use and contains 10% magnesium, which is adequate. It is advisable to apply Epsom salt to the whole garden once a year in spring at a rate of a tablespoon per shrub or 60 $g/m^2$. Do this only if deficiency symptoms are present.

**Q: For what purpose should the following chemicals be used and what are their recommended rates: ammonium sulphate; copper sulphate; ferrous sulphate; manganese sulphate; and zinc oxide?**
A: **Ammonium sulphate:** A nitrogen fertiliser which causes the ammonia nitrogen to be converted to nitrates, a process which can take up to four weeks in cool weather. It also contains a useful amount of sulphur. It is generally used for leafy crops at a rate of 30 $g/m^2$ every four to six weeks during the active growing season. Remember always to water well after each application as it can burn the foliage if not dissolved quickly. It has a slight soil-acidifying effect and can be used on alkaline soils. It can also be used as a compost activator.
**Copper sulphate:** It is sometimes used to correct copper deficiency in poor, acid, sandy and peat-rich soils. Rates vary but 2,5 $g/12 \, m^2$ has been used.
**Ferrous sulphate:** This is used to correct chlorosis in acid-loving plants like azaleas. Dissolve 10 g chelated compound in 10 litres of water and water plants at a rate of 5 litres/$m^2$. The soil should be moist before application.
**Manganese sulphate:** Manganese is a trace element and is only needed in very small quantities by plants to form proteins. Deficiency symptoms are likely on alkaline soils and show up as yellowing of younger leaves between the veins. Apply in a trace element mixture at label-recommended rates.
**Zinc oxide:** Zinc is another trace element and is important as an enzyme activator. Deficiency symptoms are leaf mottling and yellowing of younger leaves and are likely to occur on very acid and very alkaline soils. It should be used with caution and can be applied at a rate of two tablespoons/$m^2$. It must not be used on alkaline and lime-rich soils.

**Q: What is loam and how can I recognise it?**
A: Loam is soil that contains more or less equal parts of clay, sand and silt with lots of organic matter. Loamy soil is friable, fertile and moisture-retentive but drains well. Any soil will benefit and improve with regular additions of well-rotted organic matter.

**Q: How does one recognise the nutritional value of natural soil?**

A: The nutritional value of soil is hard to determine by casual inspection. Soil will have to be analysed by a laboratory to determine the nutritional value, after which recommendations can be made on a fertiliser programme specifically for your garden.

**Q: Our soil is very sandy. How can we grow shrubs and trees?**
A: Sandy soil needs good loam and plenty of organic matter. Add a layer of loam about 5 cm thick and lots of organic matter such as manure, compost or peat moss. Green manure crops will also help. Dig this into the sand to a depth of about 30 cm. Apply a complete fertiliser at regular intervals during the growing season. When planting trees and shrubs, large holes should be prepared and filled with good loam, compost and complete fertiliser. Mulch established plants to improve water retention and reduce water usage.

**Q: What is the quickest way of bringing an old garden back into production so that plants will flourish again?**
A: Work in lots of organic matter like manure and compost during autumn and spring. Apply superphosphate and complete fertiliser at a rate of 60 g/m². Keep the soil well mulched and fertilise at regular intervals.

**Q: The soil in my garden gets hard and dry on the surface but stays wet beneath the surface. What can I do?**
A: You have a clay soil that does not drain well. To improve the situation incorporate coarse sand and compost into the upper layer.

**Q: Is moss an indication of acid soil?**
A: No, moss will grow on both acid and alkaline soils that are usually low in fertility and high in moisture.

**Q: Why is lime used for soil improvement?**
A: Lime contains calcium which is an important element for cell strengthening and root development. It counteracts acidity, helps to decompose organic matter faster, aids in the development of nitrogen-fixing bacteria and reduces the toxicity of certain chemical compounds. Wood ashes (ash from a wood or charcoal fire) are a good source of natural lime.

**Q: Which plants need lime in the soil and which do better without it?**
A: Plants that grow well on neutral to alkaline soils, such as legumes and pink hydrangeas, would grow well with additions of lime. Acid-loving plants like azaleas, rhododendrons, camellias, blue hydrangeas, ferns, etc. need no lime, but they do require calcium. Lime should only be applied to very acid soils with a pH of 5,5 and lower, as most plants prefer a slightly acid soil with a pH of 6,0 to 6,9.

**Q: How does one fertilise plants that remain in the same spot in the garden?**
A: Apply the fertiliser by scattering it evenly over the surface and working it in lightly without disturbing or injuring the roots of the plants. Water thoroughly after application.

**Q: What are plant growth regulators?**
A: Plant growth regulators are hormones and are useful in aiding the quick development of roots on cuttings. Some are used to increase flower formation and others are used to increase the keeping quality of fruits and vegetables in storage.

**Q: How does one colour-treat hydrangeas to get a more intense blue colour?**
A: The colour of most hydrangea blooms depends on the soil pH. The more acid, the more intense the blue and the more alkaline, the stronger the pink. A pH of 5,0 is adequate for an intense blue colour. You can lower the pH by using either iron chelate, flowers of sulphur or diluted aluminium sulphate to maintain or increase the blue colour. Mulch with peat moss, pine needles or acid compost. The blue colouring is due to aluminium being taken up by the plant, changing the flowers from pink to blue or red to purple. Aluminium can only be used by the plant in acidic soil.

# organic gardening

As a result of people becoming more health- and nature-conscious, organic gardening has gained in popularity in recent years. It simply means a return to more natural practices without using any refined chemicals like fertilisers, fungicides, growth regulators, pesticides and herbicides which have harmful side effects on nature by leaving residues in soils, water, crops and the atmosphere. The ecosystem is a living organism, and interfering with just one aspect will affect the whole system.

In organic gardening one strives to keep the soil healthy and apply crop rotation, companion planting and biological control. It is thus very important to put as much organic matter as possible back into the soil and control weeds by mulching and removing them physically, as they may be hosts to pests and diseases. All diseased plant material will also have to be burnt to avoid contaminating the compost heap. Stressed and weak plants are also much more susceptible to pests and diseases and should be avoided by making the correct plant choices for one's area right from the start.

## Keeping the soil healthy

Organic matter is the key to healthy and fertile soil, alive with micro-organisms and earthworms. To achieve an ideal soil structure, therefore, one will have to maintain a high level of organic matter in the soil, which will encourage micro-organisms to supply nutrients to plant roots. Mulch your soil regularly to avoid bare soil patches exposed to the sun, and do not cultivate the soil too much. Organic matter also improves the soil texture and moisture retention.

Nitrogen is one of the most important plant nutrients as it is the key element in many metabolic processes. Scientific evidence has shown that if the organic matter in soil is used as a source of nitrogen, all the other elements will be made available in the correct ratios. By using refined nitrogen fertilisers one causes a temporary overdose which, in its turn, causes a temporary imbalance in the availability of other elements.

If as much organic matter as possible can be put back into the soil, the nitrogen reserve will be ample for plants to draw on. Plants can then depend on this reserve for a balanced nutrient supply which will improve the nutritional quality of crops. Since the food value of organic plant matter on its own is low, the addition of organic fertilisers is essential to ensure correct feeding of plants.

The three major macronutrients essential for all plant growth are nitrogen (N), phosphorus (P) and potassium (K). Nitrogen is necessary to maintain healthy green leaf growth, phosphorus is essential for good root development and potassium is needed to encourage flower and fruit formation. Secondary macronutrients are magnesium (Mg), calcium (Ca) and sulphur (S), and occur naturally in most soils.

Micronutrients or trace elements are necessary in very small quantities. These are iron (Fe), zinc (Zn), manganese (Mn), boron (B), molybdenum (Mo) and copper (Cu). They are included in plant food formulations like Nitrosol, Seagro and Kelpak.

Organic fertilisers rich in nitrogen are dried blood, hoof-and-horn meal, bone meal and composted chicken, sheep and goat manure. Other natural fertilisers include fish meal for major macronutrients, rock phosphate for phosphorus, calcium and micronutrients, bone meal for phosphorus, wood ash for potassium, gypsum and lime for calcium and seaweed meal for potassium and micronutrients.

The old practice of companion planting where flowers and vegetables are combined for special benefits, is again popular today.

## Compost

Compost-making is an economic and easy way to recycle disease-free garden waste. Keep the following in mind to make good-quality compost:

- Suitable materials for composting are all organic materials, including uncooked kitchen waste like vegetable and fruit peels, tea leaves, eggshells, nutshells, all types of manure, torn-up newspapers and cardboard boxes, flowers, leaves, sawdust, twigs, straw and lawn clippings.
- Use commercially available bins or make a wire-mesh or wooden box to make your compost in.
- Avoid using the same type of organic matter, for example just grass clippings from the lawn, as it tends to form a mat with poor aeration. Remember to layer different particle sizes. Spread organic material of the same type in 10-cm-thick layers, starting with carbon material such as wood shavings and twigs, followed by nitrogenous material like lawn clippings and leaves and a compost activator. Repeat this layering effect as the heap builds up.
- Compost activators are micro-organisms that break down the organic matter. They can be introduced by adding animal manure, some compost from your previous compost heap or commercially available compost activators.
- The correct temperature range is necessary for composting. The rate of decomposition is much faster during the hot and humid summer months.
- Organisms need oxygen and moisture to decompose organic matter. A badly aerated compost heap has an unpleasant smell. The compost heap should be damp but not soggy. Turn the heap over every two to three weeks to help with aeration.
- To have a nutrient-rich compost one must add organic-derived plant food in the form of animal manure to the heap.
- Under ideal conditions, compost should be ready after six weeks.

## Green manure

Green manure is another inexpensive way to get organic matter into the soil. It is especially useful on light, sandy soils. By this method a crop is grown on the site where organic matter is needed and worked directly into the ground without having to go through the decomposing process first. Legumes can also be cut down and left as a mulch on the ground. Ideal green manure plants are legumes like lupins, cowpeas, beans, clover or alfalfa, or cereal grains such as oats or Italian rye-grass. These plants are grown for a season and cut down to be worked into the ground when the first flowers appear, before seeds are formed.

One of the best methods of producing compost is simply to deposit suitable materials on an open, aerated heap, which is turned regularly.

## Mulching

Mulching is important for the following reasons:
- It adds organic matter to depleted soil.
- It increases microbial activity.
- It protects the soil from harsh sunlight and soil erosion.
- It helps to preserve moisture, thus reducing the need for irrigation.
- It helps with weed control.
- It acts like a blanket to protect plants from cold damage.
- It makes the garden look neat, tidy and well cared for.
- It increases crop production and helps to grow chemical-free food with a higher nutrient value.

Materials suitable for mulching are compost, peat moss, grass clippings, leaves, straw, bark chips, sawdust, wood shavings, nutshells, decomposed animal manure and pine needles. Fresh materials like green grass clippings should be left to dry in the sun before use. Also remember to add nitrogen in the form of manure or organic fertiliser, to prevent nitrogen deficiency. As a rule, it is better to use decomposed plant material. Nitrogen-fixing plants such as legumes can be planted as a mulch to help boost the natural nitrogen source in the soil.

# Pest and disease control

The following methods can be used to good effect to protect your plants from pests and diseases.

## Crop rotation

Problems occur if the same type of plant is grown in the same soil year after year. Pests and diseases that thrive on a particular crop can easily multiply to large proportions. Nematodes (eelworms) are a well-known example of this, and planting marigolds is a good way of getting rid of these pests. Crop rotation, biological control and the breeding of resistant varieties are the only solutions to this problem. Different plant types attract different pests, so by rotating legumes, root crops and leafy crops pests will not have enough time to multiply and become a serious problem.

## Companion plants

By simulating nature in having a variety of different plants growing together, one can avoid problems with pests and diseases. Some plants attract beneficial insects, for instance parasitic wasps, while others, for example nasturtiums, will deter harmful insects. Companion planting also means grouping plants with different root lengths and light requirements together.

Some examples of good companions are: tomatoes with onions, marigolds, basil and nasturtiums; strawberries with spinach, leeks, garlic, beans and lettuce; cabbage with onions, beetroot, celery, herbs and potatoes. Use indigenous wild garlic as a companion for cabbage, tomatoes, lettuce and squash. Marigolds are an excellent companion for roses, fruit trees and most vegetables. Garlic is a wonderful insect deterrent as well as a fungicide. Take note that the following do not make good companions: carrots with dill, and cabbage with tomatoes, runner beans or strawberries.

## Biological control

This is the introduction or encouragement of natural predators and pathogens to suppress certain insect pests. The ladybird beetle is a well-known example of predator control of aphids. Other commonly known beneficial insects are the praying mantis, many spiders and parasitic wasps, to name but a few. It is very important to be able to identify insects and their various stages of development, so that beneficial ones can be distinguished from enemy ones. Shelter and a continuous supply of food will have to be provided for them if they are to patrol your garden continuously.

## Questions and answers

**Q: Which natural insecticides and pesticides can I use in my garden?**
A: There are ready-made commercially available organic insecticides: one is called Natural Insecticide, manufactured by Efekto, and the other is Naturen Rape Oil Insecticide. These should be used once pests are present as they kill only on contact. They are effective for use on aphids, mealybug and red spider mite.
Home-made remedies include:

■ Garlic tea used as a spray will repel aphids, spider mites, whiteflies, carrot flies and mealybug. It also contains an antifungal component. Make garlic tea by blending two whole bulbs of garlic with two red chillies and one cup of water. Strain and make up a concentrate by adding water to make 2 litres. Dilute one cup of concentrate in 2 litres of water to spray onto plants.

■ Soap spray can be prepared by adding 5 ml of dishwashing liquid to 1 litre of water. Use this spray to control aphids and mealybug.

■ Nasturtium spray. To make up this spray, pour two cups of boiling water over two handfuls of fresh nasturtium leaves and steep for 15 minutes. Dilute ten drops of this tea in 1 litre of water to control aphids and red spider mite. For scale insects, dilute 100 ml of the tea in 1 litre of water and spray.

■ Wormwood (*Artemisia absinthium*) or tansy (*Tanacetum vulgare*) spray. Prepare a concentrate by pouring 2 litres of boiling water over 300 g fresh wormwood or 30 g dried wormwood. Steep for 15 minutes and strain. Dilute 20 ml concentrate in 1 litre of water and spray against cutworm, bollworm, fruit flies, rust and mildew.

■ Bitterwood (*Quassia amara*) extract. Prepare a concentrate by soaking 200 g of quassia chips in 2 litres of water for 12 hours. Bring to a quick boil and strain. Use this extract as a general insect poison. (Quassia chips and dried wormwood are available in health shops.)

**Q: Is Jeyes Fluid harmful if used to disinfect the soil?**
A: Yes; it is quite a powerful disinfectant which kills all beneficial micro-organisms as well as harmful organisms in the soil.

**Q: What is leaf mould and where does one use it?**
A: Leaf mould is made of decomposed leaves. It is made by stacking damp leaves and soil in alternate layers. Decomposition takes a very long time – up to 12 months. Leaf mould makes excellent potting soil, especially for ferns.

**Q: I am told that planting by the moon will improve productivity. How does this influence ordinary gardening activities?**
A: We all know that the moon has a profound effect on tidal movement and on the weather. The same holds true for plants. Planting by the moon means that we use the different moon phases to our advantage.

Nasturtiums and vegetables are good companion plants as nasturtiums deter harmful insects.

**During the full-moon phase:** Sow green-manure crops for mulching, fertilise plants for optimum absorption, harvest fruit and vegetables just after full moon for tastier crops and better storage ability, and plant root crops two to three days after full moon. The best time for sowing is three days before and seven days after full moon. Do not cultivate the soil and do not prune any plants during the full-moon phase. Rain is also a possibility during this time.

**During the waxing-moon phase:** Plant fruits, vegetables and flowers that produce above ground, cultivate the soil and mow the lawn for a lush appearance. Do not plant potatoes and beans, and do not feed plants during this phase. This is also not a good time to harvest fruits and herbs, and pest control on crops will also not be very effective.

**During the new-moon phase:** Prune and trim plants and control pests and diseases for optimum effect. Do not harvest fruit and vegetables and avoid sowing during this phase.

**During the waning-moon phase:** This is the best time to feed and water plants for optimum absorption. Do not plant and sow during this phase.

**Q: How can dried manure instead of rotted manure be used?**
A: It is very useful as a compost activator and can be mixed into the soil in the vegetable and flower gardens.

**Q: What plants and trees benefit by an application of wood ash?**
A: Almost all plants that need potash, such as fruit trees, root vegetables, hydrangeas, carnations, roses and peonies etc., would benefit from wood ash.

**Q: Is sawdust good to use as a mulch?**
A: Yes, if additional nitrogen is added to prevent nitrogen loss from the soil while it is decomposing. However, where termites (white ants) are present sawdust attracts them to the garden.

**Q: Does dog and cat manure have any value as a fertiliser?**
A: Dog manure is high in nitrogen and should be mixed with compost before using. Cat litter can also be used to aid the decomposition process of the compost heap. Do not use fresh as it can burn the plants.

**Q: Do any plants other than legumes and green-manure crops supply nitrogen to the soil?**
A: Any plant material that is worked into the ground does supply a certain amount of nitrogen. However, the proportions vary with different types of plants.

Spiders, as well as the praying mantis (opposite page), are good examples of biological control, as they are natural predators of many insects.

**Q: How can poultry manure be used to best advantage? I'm told that it is too strong to use in the garden.**
A: Poultry manure is excellent for making compost as it is not likely to burn any plants this way. It can be used to make liquid manure, which is very good for leafy vegetable crops. It can also be dried and crushed to a powder, which can be sprinkled thinly onto the soil and dug into the ground. It contains roughly 3-5% nitrogen, 2,5–3,5% phosphate and up to 1,7% potassium.

**Q: I am told that dried and crushed eggshells are good for the soil. Is this true?**
A: Yes, they are beneficial as they contain calcium. The best way to utilise them would be to scatter them onto the compost heap.

**Q: Do large quantities of mixed leaves make good fertiliser when decomposed?**
A: No. They have little fertiliser value on their own, but they are an excellent soil conditioner and will make the soil temporarily acid if used in large quantities.

# lawns

One of the most satisfying sights in a garden is a well-kept lawn. It has always been the best way to cover and maintain large areas of the garden quickly and at a relatively low cost. A lawn allows the house to blend with the garden, softens harsh outlines and complements trees, shrubs, perennial and annual borders. It reduces the temperature and glare on hot summer days to give a feeling of spacious coolness. It is an ideal surface on which to walk, lie, play and relax.

As the lawn is a permanent feature of the garden, extra care should be taken when choosing and establishing a particular lawn. Regular mowing, watering and feeding are the main prerequisites for a green and lush-looking lawn.

Until recently little thought has been given to the lawn's great need for water. It is important to choose a grass that is indigenous to your locality as these grasses are more drought-tolerant than exotic varieties. Another alternative to a water-demanding lawn would be to reduce the lawn surface by areas of ground covering or gravel, paving or drought-tolerant ground covers that take no traffic.

When establishing a new lawn, avoid areas that are exposed to heavy traffic by people and pets and keep away from doorways, corners, heavily shaded areas and steep slopes which would be difficult to mow. Do not plant a lawn in small areas and remember to shape the lawn area in flowing lines which are easier to mow and water than sharp corners. Your choice of lawn grass depends on your climate. There are two basic types of lawn grasses – cool-season and subtropical grasses.

## Cool-season grasses

These can withstand cold winters but do not tolerate hot, dry summers. They need plenty of water to stay green and are usually started from seeds. Seeds are sold in blends of several different grasses or as individual types. All Season's Evergreen by Mayford is an example of a cool-season grass. It grows in full sun or dappled shade and has a bunch-type, tuft-forming growth habit compared to the creeping nature of Kikuyu or Cynodon, so that edge trimming is reduced. Shade-over is a mixture of shade-tolerant grasses, specifically developed for bare patches in shade areas. Leisure Lawns is another example of a bunch-type grass. These lawns are never scarified or top-dressed and are also mowed higher than runner-type lawns.

## Subtropical grasses

Warm-season grasses grow vigorously during hot weather and are dormant in cold winters. These are usually grown from runners, plugs or sods and very seldom from seeds. The most common are Kikuyu, Berea or LM, Country Club, Buffalo grass or Cynodon-type grasses like Bayview, Gulfgreen, Florida, Tifgreen and Skaapplaas.

A beautiful expanse of well-maintained lawn is one of the most satisfying sights in a garden.

# Table of different runner-type grasses available

| Variety | Frost-free Coastal | Frost-free Winter rainfall | Severe frost | Light frost | Semi-shade |
|---|---|---|---|---|---|
| Berea or LM (*Dactyloctenium australe*) | X | X | | X | X |
| Bermuda 'Jackpot' (*Cynodon dactylon* var.) | X | X | | X | |
| Buffalo (*Stenotaphrum secundatum*) | X | X | | X | |
| Kearsney (*Axonopus compressus*) | X | | | X | X |
| Country Club (*Paspalum vaginatum*) | X | X | | | |
| Silverton Blue (*Cynodon dactylon* var.) | X | X | | | |
| Harrismith (*Cynodon dactylon* var.) | | | X | X | |
| Newmix Sahara (*Cynodon dactylon* var.) | | | | X | |
| Bayview (*Cynodon transvaalensis* var.) | X | X | X | X | |
| Florida (*Cynodon transvaalensis* var.) | X | X | X | X | |
| Gulfgreen (*Cynodon transvaalensis* var.) | X | X | | X | X |
| Skaapplaas (*Cynodon transvaalensis* var.) | X | | X | X | |
| Tifgreen (*Cynodon transvaalensis* x *C. dactylon* hybr.) | X | X | | X | |
| Tifway (*Cynodon transvaalensis* x *C. dactylon* hybr.) | X | X | | X | |
| Tifdwarf or LMG (*Cynodon transvaalensis* x *C. dactylon* hybr.) | | | X | X | |

Kikuyu (*Pennisetum clandestinum*) is not indigenous but comes from Kenya. It is a very invasive grass and should no longer be planted as there are many better varieties available countrywide. Plus factors are that it grows aggressively and recovers rapidly after damage, is easy to grow and responds very well to feeding, can withstand heavy traffic and is excellent for erosion control on slopes. On the negative side, it needs a lot of sun and does not grow well in shade, becomes dormant in winter in cool areas, is very invasive and creates problems in flowerbeds and by invading the banks of natural streams; it also has the ability to consume large amounts of water.

Gulfgreen (*Cynodon transvaalensis* strain) is indigenous. It is drought-tolerant and needs much less water than Kikuyu, and it can withstand saline conditions very well. It grows more vigorously than other Cynodon grass types, is resistant to weeds, withstands traffic very well, requires less mowing than most grasses, is frost-tolerant, remains green for longer periods than Kikuyu and is also more shade-tolerant than Kikuyu.

Bermuda 'Jackpot' (*Cynodon dactylon* var.) is indigenous. It has excellent heat and drought tolerance and needs half the amount of water that Kikuyu does to survive. It has very good disease resistance and is established quickly from seed.

## Soil preparation

The best time of year to establish a new lawn is in spring and autumn. The success of the lawn will depend on the effort you put into soil preparation. Grass will grow on almost any soil as long as it is well drained and slightly acid with a pH level of between 5,5 and 6,5. In heavy rainfall areas where the soil is acid, agricultural lime must be added at a rate of 250 g/m². Dig over the soil to a depth of 30 cm with lots of compost so that it will be able to retain water for longer periods. Kraal manure should be avoided as weeds will become a problem at a later stage. At the same time, spread superphosphate, a high-phosphorus granular fertiliser, at a rate of 90 g/m² or use bone meal at a rate of 100 g/m². Finally, spread 2:3:2 (22) at a rate of 60 g/m² or use Wonder Planting and Vegetables and rake well into the top layer of the soil. Give the soil a good soaking and leave it to settle for a few weeks. If weeds are present they will have had time to grow and can be treated with a registered weedkiller, used at recommended rates.

Before sowing or planting runners, plugs or sods the soil has to be raked until it is smooth and flat, free of clods and high and low areas.

## Seed sowing

1. A few days before sowing, soak the soil well with a fine sprinkler. Mark off the area in 1 m squares and sow the seed on a calm day.
2. To ensure correct and even distribution of seed, spread the required amount of seed over each square.
3. Sow in two directions at right angles to each other. Rake the area very lightly to incorporate the seed with the soil and roll to compact.
4. Water with a fine sprinkler to prevent runoff.

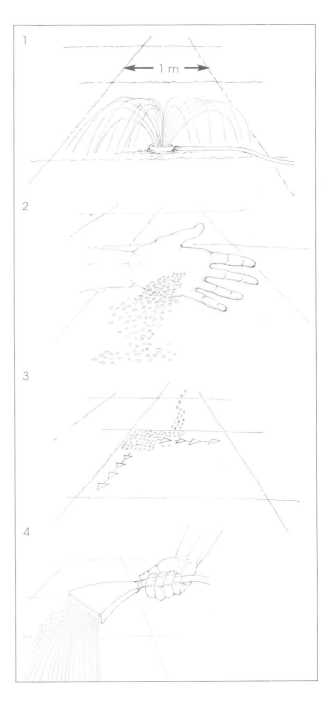

The soil surface must be kept moist constantly until complete germination has taken place, when watering may gradually be reduced. Germination will take two to three weeks, depending on the climate. First mowing will be necessary after two to three months when the grass is taller than 5 cm. Mixes like All Season's Evergreen and Shade-over should be cut no shorter than 4 cm in the sun and no shorter than 6 cm in the shade.

## Runners, plugs and sods

To establish runners, make shallow furrows about 6 cm deep and 10 cm apart for fine grass types and 15 cm apart for coarser grass types like Buffalo. Lay the runners in the furrow and rake level. Water regularly until the grass is growing. Start mowing as soon as the grass gets long; about three to four weeks after planting, depending on the weather.

Plugs should be planted in holes large enough to accommodate the plugs, spacing them evenly in a zigzag pattern. Keep moist until grass starts to spread and mow when necessary. Water regularly during hot dry weather.

Instant lawn can be established in the form of sods. This is an expensive method but provides an instant lawn with little danger of erosion or loss of planting material. It is an ideal method for sloping sites. The soil must be moist before rolling out instant lawn. Place sods to fit snugly against one another and fill gaps between them with dry sandy soil. Tramp or roll the sods after laying and water well.

## Caring for an established lawn

August is traditionally the time of year to spring-clean your lawn in the summer rainfall regions. This is the time to get your lawnmower overhauled and the blades sharpened.

It is also time to scarify the lawn if the mat build-up – often called thatch build-up – is considerable. This is only done on Kikuyu and certain Cynodon types of lawns, never on bunch-type lawns like All Season's Evergreen or Shade-over. To scarify the lawn you have to cut the lawn with the lowest setting on your lawnmower. The lawn is cut low enough if stolons (runners) are exposed and bare earth is visible. Rake or sweep up the cut material and use it for composting. One of the reasons for scarifying the lawn is to enable fertiliser to reach the roots more effectively, and another reason is to destroy the habitat of crickets, lawn caterpillars and worms. Cut the lawn at normal height if it does not have a thick mat.

After the lawn has been cut it is time to aerate the soil, especially where compaction has been caused by traffic. Aeration helps water, air and nutrients to reach the root zone. This can be done manually, using an ordinary heavy-duty garden fork, spiked roller or a special hollow-tined garden fork. Walk over the area and push the fork into the soil every 10 cm to a depth of about 15 cm.

If the lawn has been scarified, start fertilising with superphosphate or 2:3:2 (22) at a rate of 60 g/m² and water deeply immediately afterwards. If no scarifying has been necessary, fertilise with 3:2:1 (28) SR at a rate of 45 g/m² or, alternatively, use Wonder Lawns and Foliage at a rate of 60 g/m². Follow up every application of fertiliser with thorough watering. Fertilising can be repeated every six weeks alternating between 3:2:1 (28) SR and LAN at a rate of 30 g/m².

Top-dressing is necessary to fill in hollows and to level uneven areas, but never put a layer thicker than 3 cm at a time over the lawn. Remember that bunch-type lawns cannot be top-dressed. Water well after top-dressing and keep the topsoil moist until the grass shoots are growing well.

Most established lawns need 20 to 30 mm of water every week. Soil types differ, however, and sandy soils dry out quicker and will need more frequent watering than heavy loam or clay soils. During very hot or windy days, most gardens will need an extra sprinkling of water. It is important to give a long and deep soak during watering to encourage roots to develop deeper down where the soil is cooler and where the moisture content remains relatively constant.

A newly mown lawn is one of the most satisfying sights in the garden. To make mowing easier and more enjoyable one should use the correct mower, suited to the type of grass and size of lawn. Rotary mowers are best for Kikuyu, Buffalo grass and

Regular mowing, watering and feeding are the main prerequisites for a green and lush-looking lawn.

mixes like Shade-over. Cylinder- or drum-type mowers are more suitable for fine-textured lawns like Kweek or Cynodon. Mow the lawn when dry; if it is cut while damp, it is more susceptible to fungal infection. The mower blades should also be sharp. Blunt blades tear and bruise the grass so that the tips turn brown. Always mow at regular intervals. Grass which is allowed to grow too long will look patchy when it is eventually mown. The height to which grass is cut depends on what type it is. As a general rule, it is ideal to remove one-third of the leaf with each mowing.

Where weeds are a problem the best method of combating them is to use an appropriate herbicide (weed-killer). Herbicides should always be applied before weeds have gone to seed and three to four weeks after the lawn has been fertilised. Never spray herbicide on a windy day as spray drift can cause severe damage to garden plants. There are a number of selective weedkillers; consult your local nurseryman to select the correct herbicide for your specific weeds and type of grass.

If lawn is well maintained and gets enough light, it will also grow well under trees.

In the summer rainfall areas, keep a lookout for crickets, harvester termites and army worm and deal promptly with these insects. In the winter rainfall areas, moles and fungal infections are the greatest problems. To prevent fungal disease, always water during the morning so that the leaves are dry by nightfall.

It is well worth spending time and money on your lawn since you have to live with it every day. Taking that extra care brings its own rewards.

## Questions and answers

**Q: What is daisy lawn?**
A: Daisy lawn or *Lippia nodiflora* is a ground cover and comes from the USA. It is a very good substitute for lawn on sandy areas in full sun and can tolerate short periods of drought. Flowers appear during spring and attract bees; if these should cause problems the flowers can be cut off by running the lawnmower over the area.

**Q: Can lawn clippings be used in the garden?**
A: Yes, lawn clippings can be used as a mulch if scattered in thin layers and allowed to dry before adding the next layer. Add nitrogen fertiliser to prevent nitrogen loss from the soil when grass clippings decompose. The best way to utilise clippings would be to make compost by mixing them with other organic matter and use this compost as mulch.

**Q: My lawn is infested with lawn caterpillars. How should I treat my lawn to rid it of this problem?**
A: The lawn must be scarified during August to remove all the dead grass in which caterpillars can hide. Aerate, fertilise and water well. At the first sign of caterpillars use one of the following pesticides on the infested areas only: Chlorpirifos, Dursban, Garden Ripcord, Karbaspray, Malasol or Malathion, or use Wonder fertiliser 4:1:1 (21) + Karbaspray. Follow the instructions on the packet carefully. These caterpillars are active during the night, and to check whether there are any left one can leave a damp sack on the infected area overnight. By turning the sack over in the morning caterpillars will be revealed if there are any left alive.

**Q: A large patch of my lawn has turned a light blue colour and is starting to dry up. Is it a fungus?**
A: The symptoms match a fungus called brown patch. Treat this by aerating the area and watering the infected area with Benlate (active ingredient benomyl). Water the lawn with Bravo 500 at a rate of 10 litres spray mixture per 100 m² at weekly intervals as a preventative measure after symptoms appear and do not water the lawn during the afternoon,

as the fungus is more likely to attack when the grass is wet in hot and humid weather.

**Q: Is it possible to allow the lawn to grow right up to the stems of trees and palms instead of making basins around them?**
A: Yes, one can do so as long as the grass, trees and palms are fed regularly and the stems of trees and palms are not damaged by cutting the grass around them.

**Q: I should like some advice on the growing of Buffalo grass.**
A: Buffalo grass (sometimes called St. Augustine) is indigenous to our coastal areas and can easily be established by plugs. Follow the directions for soil preparation on page 37 and the establishing of runners, plugs and sods on page 38. Once established, Buffalo lawn only needs to be watered once every 14 days in dry weather. It is a low-maintenance grass ideal for frost-free or light-frost areas, especially the Western Cape.

**Q: I am told that my lawn has fairy ring. What is this?**
A: It is a fungus that causes the grass to die off in distinctive rings. Darker rings show up because of extra nitrogen released by decomposed dead leaves. Aerate the rings and water with 10 litres Bravo 500 mixture per 100 m² twice within one week and follow a preventative programme afterwards.

**Q: What can I use for Parktown prawns (mole crickets) on my lawn?**
A: Use Sluggem bait and scatter lightly at a rate of 500 g/100 m².

**Q: Is Wonderlawn a good choice for growing between stepping stones?**
A: Wonderlawn (*Dichondra repens*) is a creeping ground cover which stays evergreen in areas where mowing is a problem. It is excellent between stepping stones and pavers or in shady areas where ordinary lawn does not grow well. It is not drought-tolerant and can become invasive if not kept in check. It is very easily established by sowing seeds in the area where needed. Grows best in areas with lower humidity.

**Q: Which weedkiller can I use for broadleaf weeds in my established lawn?**
A: There are two herbicides for this purpose: one is Turfweeder APM and the other Hormoban APM. Follow instructions carefully for application rates and methods.

**Q: What grass-like ground covers can be planted instead of grass?**
A: *Dymondia margaretae (silver carpet), Festuca, Mondo grass (*Ophiopogon* spp.), *Zoysia tenuifolia* (Korean moundgrass), *Armeria maritima*, *Koeleria glauca* (bubble grass), *Sisyrinchium* 'E.K. Balls', *Minuartia verna* (Irish moss), *Acorus* spp. and *Liriope* varieties. Remember that none of these lawn substitutes can carry heavy traffic – in other words, you can't let children or animals play on them.

**Q: There are a few hollows in my lawn. How can I fill them without having to replant afterwards?**
A: It is very easy to rectify this problem. Make sure that the soil is moist before starting with the following procedure: Use a flat spade and cut a cross in the lawn, with the centre in the middle of the hollow. Carefully peel back the lawn by cutting under it with the spade so that a square of exposed soil is opened up in the hollow. Level the area by filling it with sandy, compost-enriched soil and firm gently. Fold the lawn flaps back over the bare soil and make sure that the level is corrected before watering the area thoroughly.

# seedlings

For year-round colour in the garden the use of annuals, biennials and perennials is essential. The easiest and most popular way of raising annuals is by buying seedlings from garden centres and nurseries. Many new hybrid varieties that cater for every situation are available in seed packets and are not always obtainable as seedlings from your local nursery. Your only access to these new and exciting plants would be to raise your own, which can be very rewarding if you go about it the right way. It is also the most cost-effective way to obtain plants in quantity.

Perennials provide a low-maintenance colour display and live much longer than annuals and biennials. Perennials are herbaceous plants, some of which may die down every winter and produce new stems and foliage each spring, while others keep on growing year after year. Most need to be lifted and divided every few years to keep them vigorous and prolific. Some have a limited life span and are best propagated annually as seedlings; examples are aquilegia, anchusa, coreopsis, gaillardia, geum, perennial flax, balloon flower, lupins and primulas.

Before buying seeds you will have to plan carefully in order to achieve optimum results. Ask yourself the following questions: Will it grow well in the position I have in mind? How tall will it grow? When will it flower and for how long? How fresh are the seeds? By reading the description on each seed packet you'll be able to make the right choice, making your garden more interesting with new varieties and uncommon plants. Keep a gardening diary with notes of successes and failures so that planning for the next season will become easier with each consecutive year.

## Seed sowing

The best way of raising seedlings is by sowing seeds into seed trays or boxes, seedbeds or directly into the garden (in situ), depending on the variety.

## Sowing into containers

Make sure that the container is clean before filling it with the sowing mix. The best sowing mix is a compost-based mix which is friable and well drained. Make up your own sowing mix by mixing one part by volume of good garden soil, one part washed coarse sand and two parts peat or compost. This mixture should be sterilised by either pouring boiling water over it or baking it in the oven at 60 °C for ten minutes. To each 10-litre bucketful of this mix add a tablespoon of superphosphate or bone meal, and mix well into the sowing mix.

Petunias are excellent annuals to provide year-round colour in the garden.

Fill the seed tray up to 1 cm from the rim, firming the mixture down with a firming board. Water with a copper-based fungicide like Virikop or Fongarid to prevent damping-off disease, which causes seedlings to wilt and die due to fungus. Label the tray with the name of the variety and the date. Check the sowing depth on the seed packet. A general rule is to cover the seeds with a layer of sowing mix twice their depth, but very fine seeds are sown just on the surface. A good idea is to mix finer seeds with a little dry sand to ensure an even spread before scattering them thinly onto the sowing mix. Cover lightly if necessary and firm down gently. Cover the container with clear plastic or glass to maintain an even moisture level and temperature. Place in a warm, light position out of direct sunlight and remove the cover as soon as germination is complete, to ensure ventilation. If seedlings are grown indoors on a windowsill, remember to turn the container daily to prevent seedlings from growing at a one-sided angle. Keep the sowing mix moist but not wet. Water seed trays by placing them in a shallow pan of water. As soon as seedlings reach handling size, usually with their first set of true leaves, you will need to prick them out into small pots filled with sowing mix. Keep these transplanted seedlings in light shade for a few days before moving them into a brighter position to harden them off. Water seedlings when dry, preferably early, and add diluted liquid fertiliser once a week. They should be ready to be planted out into the garden in about four weeks' time. It might also be necessary to pinch back some varieties to encourage good branching with more buds.

Beware of snails and slugs eating newly germinated seedlings. It is always advisable to put down a preventative application of snail bait around vulnerable plants.

## Sowing into seedbeds

This method is generally used for vegetables, biennials, perennials and larger-seeded annuals. When sowing into seedbeds, make sure that the soil is well drained with a fine texture; add lots of compost and half a cup of superphosphate or bone meal per m$^2$ mixed into the soil. This should be in a sunny, sheltered spot. A 25-cm-high frame covered with 30% shade cloth will be needed to shelter small seedlings from the midday sun. Water daily with a fine sprinkler. Remember to harden off seedlings by exposing them gradually to more sun as they grow bigger.

## Sowing directly into flowerbeds

Scatter a 5-cm-thick layer of compost evenly over the soil and add a handful of general fertiliser like 3:2:1 (28) SR or Wonder Planting and Vegetables 2:3:4 (21) and a handful of superphosphate or bone meal per m$^2$. Dig the flowerbed to a depth of at least 25 cm and break up all large soil lumps. Rake it flat and water with copper-based fungicide a day before sowing. Sow the seeds thinly onto damp soil and rake lightly. Water, if necessary, with a very fine spray, making sure not to wash the seeds away. Keep the soil moist but not wet. Thin out when the seedlings are large enough to handle, making sure that they are spaced at least 5 cm apart. Two weeks later, thin out again to the required spacing specified for the variety.

## Trenching

When digging a bed for plants such as sweet peas or liliums, which need a good root depth, the best method is bastard trenching:
1.  Mark out the area required with string. Divide this into strips about a metre wide and whatever length is necessary.

2. Remove the topsoil to a depth of about 25 cm in a trench about 30 cm wide and heap it at the opposite side of the bed.
3. Dig over the bottom soil, breaking it up and adding organic matter such as well-rotted kraal manure or compost, together with a sprinkling of bone phosphate.
4. When the trench is totally dug over, move your line another 30 cm and dig a trench to a depth of 25 cm, this time moving the loosened soil into the first trench.
5. Next, loosen the bottom soil in the second trench, again including your additives. At this point start your third trench, moving its topsoil into the top of the second trench, and so on until the entire bed is trenched. Finally, put the soil from your first trench on top of the soil forked in the last trench.

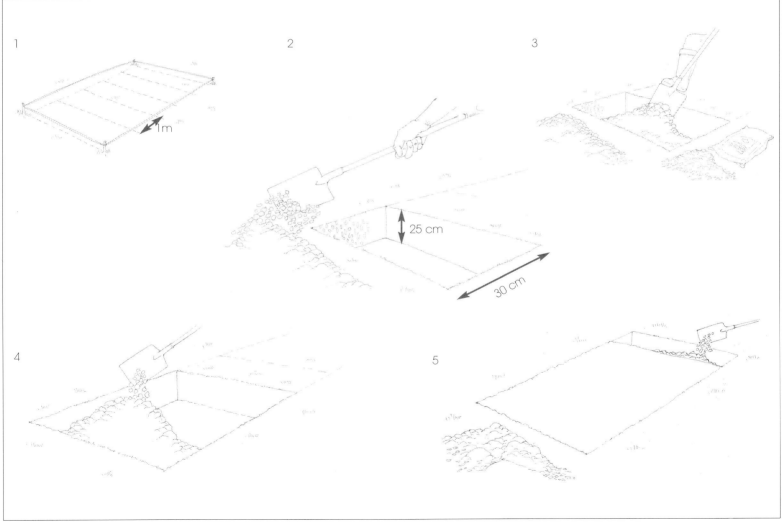

## Planting out

For planting out container-grown seedlings, prepare the soil as for sowing directly into the ground. Water both the seedlings and the planting site well the day before planting out. The best time to transplant seedlings is late in the afternoon or on a cool, overcast day. Take care to plant seedlings so that the level of soil is the same as it was in the container. Put out snail bait if necessary and water immediately and daily until the plants are well established.

## Aftercare

Once seedlings are well established and growing, a little maintenance needs to be done. Always water early in the morning so that the foliage has time to dry off before nightfall, as too much moisture during the night can encourage fungus disease. Water deeply to encourage development of deep root systems. Some light cultivation between plants may be necessary after heavy rains. The seedlings may have to be protected in winter: cover them every night with fleece cloth to prevent frost damage. Weeding has to be done on a regular basis. It is always a good idea to mulch the soil between the plants to help keep the soil moist, to keep weeds in check and to improve the soil structure by the addition of humus. Some taller-growing varieties may need staking. When flowering, annuals need to be deadheaded (the removal of spent flowers to prevent them from going to seed) regularly to encourage prolonged flowering. It is also a good idea to foliar-feed annuals once every two weeks at this stage with a weak solution of liquid organic plant food like Kelpak, Nitrosol or Bio Super Bloom to enhance performance.

## Questions and answers

**Q: What is the difference between an annual and a biennial?**
A: An annual grows from seed and then flowers and dies in one season, for example alyssum, calendula, lobelia and phlox.
   A biennial grows from seed, produces stems and leaves in one season and flowers in the next season, whereafter it dies. Examples are Canterbury bells, foxgloves, sweet William and wallflowers.

**Q: Why do my annuals no longer perform well? I grow them in the same bed every year and prepare the soil well before each planting season.**
A: It is possible that the soil in that area is overfed and needs rejuvenating. Do this by removing the top 5- to 10-cm layer of soil when preparing for the next batch of seedlings, and prepare as normal, omitting the general fertiliser until the next season. Remember, however, not to plant the same variety in the same spot year after year. Crop rotation (see page 29) applies in the flower garden as well as in the vegetable patch.

**Q: What exactly is meant by pinching back and which annuals should be pinched back?**
A: It is the removal of the tip of the growing shoot to induce branching. The following annuals can be pinched back when they are about 6–10 cm tall: coleus, cosmos, carnation, impatiens, nemesia, petunia, phlox, marigold, snapdragon, salvia, schizanthus (poor man's orchid) and verbena.

Colourful impatiens will brighten any shady corner in the garden.

**Q: Which flower seeds can be sown in situ (directly into the ground)?**

A: Anchusa, *Bokbaai vygies (*Dorotheanthus bellidiformis*), calendula, cornflower, clarkia, cosmos, coreopsis, larkspur, *Namaqualand daisy (*Dimorphotheca sinuata*), Californian poppy, godetia, baby's breath (gypsophila), sunflower, strawflower (*Helichrysum bracteatum*), candytuft, sweet pea, lavatera, linaria (toadflax), Virginian stocks, love-in-a-mist, scabious, marigold, nasturtium and meadow mixes.

**Q: I did not have much success with my petunias on the Highveld this summer. What are the best petunias to grow in hanging baskets?**

A: In the summer rainfall regions petunias perform best during winter and the drier months, as they do not like water on the flowers and are susceptible to fungus disease if overwatered or if it is very hot and humid. In the winter rainfall regions they would perform best during the hot and dry summer months. Petunias should be cut back after the first flush of flowers and fed with liquid fertiliser to prolong the flowering season. There are five main groups of petunias: grandifloras, multifloras, floribundas, millifloras and perennials. The grandifloras usually have large blooms with a vigorous growth habit and are not very weather-resistant. They are excellent for containers, hanging baskets and mass bedding displays in drier seasons. Grandiflora varieties include Supermagic, Supercascade, Falcon, Daddy, Storm, Dreams, Ultra and Fanfare Double. Multifloras produce many medium-sized flowers and are more resistant to adverse weather conditions such as wind and rain. They are ideal for mass bedding displays and rockeries. Varieties include Carpets, Primetimes, Duo doubles and Nana Compacta varieties. Floribundas combine the best features of multifloras and grandifloras and are ideal for mass bedding displays. Varieties include the Mirage series. Millifloras are small, compact plants with masses of small flowers and are ideal for window boxes, containers and bedding. Varieties include the Fantasy series. Perennials are usually longer-living, more rain- and heat-resistant and longer-flowering than the others, with masses of small flowers. They also have a cascading habit, making them ideal for hanging baskets and containers. Varieties include the Surfinias and the Million Bells series.

**Q: What are the best annuals for light shade and semi-shade positions?**

A: Alyssum, begonia, aquilegia, cineraria, coleus, Canterbury bells, forget-me-not, impatiens, linaria, lobelia, nasturtium, polyanthus, primula, Virginian stocks and wallflower.

**Q: How can I grow sweet peas for cut-flower production?**

A: To grow sweet peas successfully the soil must be well prepared. Do this about a month before the seeds need to be sown. They demand a well-drained soil with plenty of organic matter, phosphates, potash and lime. Use a fertiliser like Wonder Planting and Vegetables 2:3:4 (21) + Lime and avoid high-nitrogen fertilisers. Prepare a trench running in a north-south direction so that the plants will get the maximum amount of sun all day long. Put up a trellis at this stage. Soak the seeds for a few hours before sowing and plant them 2 cm deep, whereafter they should germinate in ten to 14 days. Be careful not to overwater at this stage, as too much moisture will cause bad germination and damping-off. Once the plants are well established they will need much more water. Pinch back small plants when they are 10–15 cm tall to encourage branching. When the first flowers appear, start feeding the plants once every three weeks with Wonder SR 3:1:5 (26) or liquid organic plant food like Nitrosol, Kelpak or Bio Super Bloom. Remember to pick flowers regularly to prolong the flowering season. The short, knee-high varieties can also be grown for cut flowers.

One of the most rewarding perennials for any garden with full sun is the day lily (*Hemerocallis* spp.), providing colour all summer long.

**Q: When is the best time to sow *Dimorphotheca sinuata* or Namaqualand daisies?**

A: Start sowing towards the end of March. Do not sow too early, as seedlings are very susceptible to fungus attack in warm, humid weather. Sowing during April and May will also be correct. Sow directly into the soil.

**Q: Which seeds can I sow during spring for summer colour and which seeds during autumn for winter and spring colour?**

A: **Annual seeds to sow during spring for summer colour are:** alyssum, amaranthus, anchusa, antirrhinum, *arctotis, aster, balsam, basil, begonia, cosmos, Canterbury bells, cornflower (centaurea), candytuft, clarkia, cleome, coleus, celosia, chrysanthemum (annual), cotula, dahlia, dianthus, Californian poppy, euphorbia (annual), globe amaranth (*Gomphrena globosa*), Gloriosa daisy (rudbeckia), godetia, gypsophila, kochia, lavatera, *lobelia, love-in-a-mist (*Nigella damascena*), lunaria, impatiens, marigold, bells of Ireland (*Molucella laevis*), mimulus, nasturtium, nicotiana, petunia, phlox, portulaca, Shirley poppy, salpiglossis, salvia, scabious, sunflower, verbena, vinca, viscaria, white lace flower (*Ammi majus*), xeranthemum, zinnia.

**Seeds to sow in autumn and mid-summer for winter colour are:** alyssum, anchusa, *arctotis, antirrhinum, *Bellis perennis*, calendula, calceolaria, candytuft, cornflower (centaurea), chrysanthemum, cineraria, blanket flower (*Gaillardia aristata*), *Bokbaai vygie (*Dorotheanthus bellidiformis*), dianthus, gomphrena, helipterum, flax (*Linum usitatissimum*), *Namaqualand or African daisy, lupins, larkspurs, lobelia, forget-me-not (*Myosotis scorpioides*), stocks, strawflower (*Helichrysum bracteatum*), sweet peas, Iceland poppy, petunia, phlox, schizanthus, sweet sultan (centaurea), verbena, viola, pansy, toadflax (linaria), nemesia, Virginian stocks, viscaria, xeranthemum. *Primula malacoides* and ornamental kale should be sown in mid-summer.

**Q: How does one divide perennials and when is the best time to do this?**

A: Many perennials become overcrowded and start to deteriorate after a few years, whereafter they need to be lifted and divided. Water the perennials that will need rejuvenating the day before dividing them. Lift the clumps and insert two garden forks back to back into the middle of the clump. Push the handles towards each other, which will divide the clump in half, or cut the clump apart with a knife or spade. This can be repeated until the clump has been divided up sufficiently. Discard old and weak shoots. Cut back the roots and upper growth by half. Keep these plants out of the direct sun to prevent the roots drying out. Prepare the bed by digging in lots of compost, manure and a handful of bone meal or superphosphate per m². Replant, mulch the area and water well. A general rule is to divide early spring-flowering varieties in autumn and late-flowering varieties in early spring. Some perennials like acanthus, peonies and helleborus need not be disturbed at all.

**Q: How and when should I divide my bearded iris plants, to ensure a lovely display of flowers for the next spring season?**

A: Bearded irises should be lifted and divided in April. Lift the clumps and shake off the soil. Prepare the soil by adding lots of organic material such as kraal manure and compost and complete fertiliser like 3:2:1 (28) SR. Remove all rotted and diseased parts. Break off new rhizomes that have developed on the sides of the central rhizome. Discard the old central rhizome. Cut off the leaves on these new divisions at about 10 cm above the rhizome. Plant on a little mound with roots hanging over the sides, cover the roots with soil and firm down. Make sure the top of the rhizome is exposed to the sun. Water well after planting.

Iceland poppies, planted here with pansies and chrysanthemums, make wonderful cut flowers in late winter and early spring.

**Q: Can I grow geraniums from seeds or can they only be propagated by slips?**

A: Yes, geraniums (*Pelargonium hortorum*) can be grown from seeds. Sow the seeds into seed trays in autumn or spring. Seeds germinate best at a temperature of 21–24 °C and should take three to seven days to emerge, whereafter it takes about 11 weeks to flower. Seeds are commercially available in a range of colours.

They can also be propagated by 10-cm-long tip cuttings which strike easily almost any time of the year, except during winter in very cold areas.

**Q: What is the difference between perennial poppies and annual poppies?**

A: Perennial or Oriental poppies (*Papaver orientale*) have hairy, mid-green toothed foliage and deep, fleshy roots. They bear showy, single, large bright-red flowers with dark blotches at the base of petals during early summer. Single and double varieties are available in colours that range from white, pink, salmon and orange to red. These poppies are best propagated by seeds sown in spring or by root cuttings in winter. Avoid disturbing the roots when transplanting seedlings.

Poppies grown as annuals in South Africa are Iceland poppies (*Papaver nudicaule*), Shirley poppies (*Papaver rhoeas*) and the opium poppy (*Papaver somniferum*). Iceland poppies are perennial but are grown as winter- and spring-flowering annuals. They have soft-green toothed foliage with hairy stems and fragrant single flowers in a variety of colours. Well-known varieties are 'Champagne Bubbles', the Wonderland series and the Giant-flowered mixtures. Seeds must be sown in late summer to autumn. Shirley poppies are fast-growing annuals with light-green lobed foliage and double flowers in shades of white, pink or red and bicolours, which appear in summer. Opium poppies are grey-foliaged annuals with large single and double flowers in shades of white, pink, red or purple, often with a dark centre.

**Q: Which annuals can be planted for a colourful display that would require not too much care?**

A: Annual phlox, alyssum, bedding begonias, cosmos, gaillardia, marigold, impatiens, *lobelia, petunia, salvia, verbena and zinnia.

**Q: How can I save the seeds from annual flowers and would they come true to their parent?**

A: Choose healthy plants and allow seeds to mature on the plant. Gather the seeds in dry weather, just before they are shed, and save them in a cool, dry place. Annual seeds to harvest would be marigolds, salvia, zinnias and Namaqualand daisies. Seeds of hybrid varieties would not come true as they would have a mixture of genetic information from both parents. Most annuals are hybridised and it would not really be worthwhile to try to save the seeds. It is much safer to buy named varieties to guarantee success. Seeds from herbs would be about the only worthwhile seeds to harvest.

**Q: What parts of foxgloves are poisonous?**

A: The drug digitalis, if taken in overdoses, is lethal. It is obtained from the second year's young leaves. All parts of the plant would probably be poisonous, with the most poison concentrated in the foliage.

**Q: When I buy seedlings from my local nursery, most of them seem to be in full flower. Does this mean that they won't flower for long in my garden?**

A: The trend today is to sell most seedlings in colour, allowing for an instant display in the garden. As long as they are deadheaded regularly the plants grow and develop normally, giving months of ongoing blooms. Some exceptions to this general rule are foxgloves, stocks, cinerarias, larkspurs and lupins, which are best planted 'green'.

Indigenous gazanias are excellent in hot, sunny positions.

**Q: I would like to grow my own flowers for drying so that I can eventually use them in arrangements. What can you suggest?**

A: There is quite a wide variety of garden plants that would be suitable for drying. You can easily include some of the following plants in existing beds and borders. The most popular flowers for drying are those with papery petals, such as strawflower (*Helichrysum bracteatum*), statice (*Limonium latifolium*) and everlasting flower (*Helipterum* spp., also called acroclinium). Ordinary border plants excellent for drying are delphinium, honesty (*Lunaria annua*), lavender (*Lavandula* spp.), bear's breeches (*Acanthus mollis*) and the sea hollies (*Eryngium* spp.). Dried seed heads of the following plants are also excellent for dried arrangements: many grasses, poppies (*Papaver* spp.), love-in-a-mist (*Nigella damascena*), onions (*Allium* spp.) and lotus (*Nelumbo nucifera*).

# bulbs

When thinking of bulbs, a beautiful spring display immediately comes to mind. Most gardeners do not realise, however, that there are many different kinds of bulbs which will adorn their gardens with beautiful flowers throughout the year. Bulbs are not only colourful, but are also very easy to grow; they make wonderful cut flowers and many have a lovely fragrance as well. Gardeners usually include several different kinds of plants in the 'bulb' category, for example corms (gladiolus, freesias, anemones, watsonias), tuberous roots (dahlias, ranunculus), tubers (potatoes, caladium, peonies, begonias), true bulbs (amaryllis, daffodils, hyacinths, liliums, onions) and rhizomes (iris, canna, arums, red-hot pokers).

In short, 'bulbs' are perennial storage organs which produce leaves, stems, flowers and roots. It is important to remember that after flowering the foliage of bulbs remains green for some time because it needs to manufacture and supply food to the bulbs, which store it for the next flowering season. Always let the foliage die down naturally before cutting it off, to ensure a successful display for the following cycle. During the dormant or rest period the new flower bud is being developed inside the bulb.

## Planting bulbs

There are two main planting seasons for bulbs: late autumn for winter- and spring-flowering varieties and spring for summer-flowering varieties. It is not difficult to grow bulbs successfully in any ordinary garden soil, provided that the soil is well drained and loosened to a depth of about 25 cm and that plants are watered well throughout their growing season. Prepare the soil by incorporating sand if the soil is heavy clay, and add compost and well-rotted manure before planting. Buy your bulbs from a reputable nursery or garden centre only and plant them at the correct time of year. Bulbs are usually packaged with full instructions on planting time, depth, spacing, light requirements and care.

Most winter- and spring-flowering bulbs need a period of cold to induce growth and flower formation; therefore you have to plant them once the soil cools down in late autumn. The summer-flowering bulbs need warmth to start growing and must be planted in spring. When planting bulbs there are a few basic principles that apply to most bulbs.

- Prepare the soil in advance and be sure to loosen it to at least 25 cm (30 cm for liliums).
- A general rule is to plant bulbs with the pointed side up at a depth of about twice the diameter of the bulb. Ranunculus must be planted with the claws facing downwards and anemone corms need to be planted with the point facing downwards.
- Winter- and spring-flowering bulbs prefer cool soil conditions and will not perform well in any hot situation.
- Space large bulbs like amaryllis 20–25 cm apart and smaller bulbs like *Muscari botryoides* (grape hyacinth) 5 cm apart.
- If moles are a problem in your garden, plant your bulbs in a wire basket.
- After planting, mulch the area with a 1–3-cm-thick layer of compost or peat. Annuals and ground covers can also be planted over the bulbs to act as living mulch; an added advantage is that they will prolong the flowering display by hiding the yellowing foliage of bulbs that are dying down.

*Clivia miniata* is one of South Africa's most beautiful bulbous plants and never fails to bring colour to the spring garden.

- Make sure the soil at root level is kept moist at all times. Water every four to five days to soak the soil to a depth of 15 cm. Increase watering in hot, dry and windy weather. If the soil is allowed to dry out it may cause bulbs to abort their flowers, preventing them from flowering at all.
- Fertilise bulbs when planting and after flowering if you intend to keep them for the next season. If you want to grow your bulbs as an annual display only and to discard them after flowering, it will not be necessary to feed them at all.
- Remove spent flowers regularly to prevent seed formation and ensure a much neater appearance. They will only sap the strength of the bulbs if you want to keep them for the next season.

## Bulbs in containers

Bulbs make a spectacular display in containers, especially in late winter when everything in the garden is looking bleak. Spring-flowering annuals such as alyssum, pansies, primulas, forget-me-not and Virginian stocks are ideal to combine with bulbs in containers. Be creative in selecting interesting colour combinations for different containers. Any container with a depth of 20 cm or more will suit most bulbs. Remember that the soil in containers tends to dry out fast in a sunny position. Place containers in a semi-shaded area to help ensure that the roots of bulbs in the container stay moist at all times. Containers with bulbs in full bloom can be brought indoors for display. Bulbs grown in containers can be treated as annuals, unless you want to keep them for the next season. You will have to keep on watering and feeding the container after flowering until the bulbs go into their rest period.

When planting up a container with bulbs, be sure to use a friable, well-drained potting mix. Mix some water-retaining granules into the potting mix before filling the container to the deepest bulb-planting depth. Water to let the soil settle. Place the bulbs on the potting mix without pressing them down and cover with potting mix to the new, shallower planting depth in case of a second type of bulb that requires a shallower depth. Fill up the container to about 2 cm below the rim to facilitate watering. Water containers regularly after planting to keep the potting mix moist at all times. Do not use drip trays under containers, as these will cause the potting mix to become waterlogged and the bulbs to rot. If drip trays are essential, be sure to empty them after the excess water has drained out. Plant annuals when the new shoots of bulbs appear. Containers should be in full colour after about five months. Feed bulb-and-annual combinations every two weeks with liquid plant food such as Multifeed P, Nitrosol or Supranure. Bulbs that are not meant to be kept for the next season do not need to be fertilised. Feed bulbs with special bulb food after flowering if you intend to keep the bulbs for the next season. Remember that hyacinths and tulips will not flower well the next season and should be discarded.

## Winter- and spring-flowering bulbs

These bulbs have their dormant period during summer and include many indigenous bulbs native to the Western Cape. Winter bulbs need lots of water, especially in the summer rainfall regions, and resent being planted too early in hot soil. The planting season for these bulbs starts during late March until early June, depending on the variety and soil temperatures. After flowering these bulbs generally can be lifted during November. Cut all foliage and dust with a fungicide before packing them in wooden crates or cardboard boxes to be stored in a dry place like the garage or garden shed. Remember to mark each variety before storing.

St Joseph's lilies (*Lilium longiflorum*) make wonderful cut flowers and have a lovely fragrance as well.

The following winter- and spring-flowering bulbs can be planted from April until mid-May: *Allium cowanni* (florist's allium), anemones, *babiana (baboon flower), *Cyrtanthus purpureus* (fire lily or George lily), daffodils or narcissus, *daubenya (jewel of the desert), Dutch iris, endymion (bluebells), *freesias, hyacinths, ipheion (spring starflower), *ixia (wand flower), *Lachenalia aloides* (Cape cowslip), *Leucojum vernum* (snowflake), *Muscari botryoides* (grape hyacinth), *Moraea neopavonia* (peacock flower), *Ornithogalum thyrsoides* (chincher-inchee), ranunculus, *sparaxis (harlequin flower), *tritonia (blazing star), tulips, *watsonias.

Plant treated tulip bulbs from the end of May until early June.

## Summer- and autumn-flowering bulbs

These bulbs have their rest period during winter, start to grow in spring, flower in summer and die down in autumn again, ready for their winter rest period. They originate from summer rainfall regions and cannot stand dry periods during summer, when they are actively growing. The best planting time for summer-flowering bulbs is from early August until late October. All summer-flowering bulbs can be lifted during May after the foliage has died down naturally, if you intend to save them for the next season. Plant all true liliums during July and August.

The following summer-flowering bulbs can be planted from August until October: Amaryllis, begonia, childan-thus (Peruvian daffodil), *Crocosmia aurea* (garden montbretia), dahlia, *Galtonia candicans* (berg lily), *gladi-olus, *Hymenocallis littoralis* (white spider lily), *Liatris pycnostachya* (gayfeather), lilium, *nerine, *Polianthes tuberosa* (tuberose), *Sinningia speciosa* (gloxinia), sprekelia (Maltese cross), *Tigridia pavonia* (tiger flower or lily), *Zantedeschia* spp.(arum lilies), *Zephyranthes grandiflora* (rain lily or zephyr lily).

## Pests and diseases

Most bulbs in the garden are relatively pest- and disease-free if you follow proper garden management princi-ples. Practise crop rotation (see page 29) to prevent soil-borne diseases from attacking bulbs like gladioli, dahlias, freesias, montbretias, liliums, Dutch irises and gayfeathers. Try to plant these bulbs in a different area of the garden or flowerbed every year. Remove weeds, which may harbour pests and diseases, regularly. Always plant bulbs within their required specifications. Keep a constant lookout for insects and diseases. Before spray-ing pesticides, identify the problem and deal with it promptly. Always follow application instructions carefully for all pesticides.

The following are the most common pests and diseases found on bulbs in the garden (see pages 143-149 for recommended control methods):

- Aphids can be a problem on liliums, tulips and other bulbs. They cause twisted, curled and discoloured foliage, resulting in poor growth.
- Cutworms usually attack summer-flowering bulbs such as dahlias, amaryllis and nerines, and any young plants.
- Fungus disease (mildew, blight and rust) is usually a problem under warm and humid conditions. Foliage may become spotted or a greyish mould may appear, causing stunted and yellow growth. Fungus can attack gladioli in the form of rust; on ranunculus, dahlias and anemones it can also appear as mildew and on tulips and liliums as blight.

A colourful display of winter- and spring-flowering bulbs.

- Leaf miners are the larval stage of leaf-miner flies that tunnel through the leaves. Dahlias and ranunculus are susceptible to this problem.
- Lily borers are caterpillars that bore into stems and leaves and later into the bulb to eat out the centre, which can cause the bulb to die. Systemic pesticides are usually very effective to control this problem.
- Mealybug causes plants to grow slowly and can be a problem on amaryllis and nerines.
- Red spider mite causes speckled, bronzed or dried-up foliage on dahlias and tuberoses.
- Snails and slugs can be a problem on young foliage.
- Thrips are small black insects which feed on the buds, flowers and foliage of gladioli, Inca lilies and amaryllis.
- Virus disease is identified by stunted growth with curled-up, distorted and discoloured flowers. Sometimes virus appears as a white-and-green-mottled pattern on foliage. Plants with virus have to be destroyed.

# Questions and answers

**Q: Could you give me some advice on how bulbs are propagated, as I would like to multiply my own bulbs?**

A: There are different methods of propagation available for different kinds of bulbs.

1. The first method would be by means of seeds. Most bulbs can be propagated in this way. It is important to remember that plants obtained through this method will not necessarily be identical to the parent plants. If parents are genetically different their offspring will be hybrids, which may differ from parent plants in colour, shape and growth habit. Sow winter bulb seeds in April and summer bulb seeds in September.
2. The second method is the easiest and involves the removal of offsets. These are baby bulbs that have developed from the base of the mother bulb. Baby bulbs can be detached and grown in the same way as adult bulbs. Corms and true bulbs both form offsets, which may be removed from mother bulbs when these are lifted and stored until the next season.
3. A third method is by means of cuttings. Here, new shoots that develop from tubers at the beginning of the season can be cut off with a piece of the tuber and rooted in a well-drained medium like washed river sand. These rooted cuttings can be grown in the soil like seedlings.
4. Leaf cuttings can be made from certain kinds of bulbs, where little bulbs form on the cut-off end of a leaf. Make leaf cuttings early in the growing season and use only healthy, fully grown leaves. Place the cut-off side of the leaf cutting about 2 cm deep into washed river sand. Little bulbs will form on the edge and can be removed once their own roots have developed.
5. Another method is through division. This method is commonly used for tubers and tuberous roots. This is done at the beginning of the bulb-growing season when eyes have started to swell. Divide tuberous roots so that each piece has at least one eye, and dust wounds with a fungicide. Let the wound dry out for a few days before planting these pieces into the garden.

**Q: We have noted some beautiful flowering bulbs in the veld. Can these be transplanted into the garden successfully?**

A: Uprooting bulbs in the wild is against the law, and disturbing bulbs during their flowering period is also not a very good idea as they will probably die after being transplanted. The best time to transplant bulbs is during their rest period. Indigenous bulbs can be obtained from various indigenous nurseries and the national botanical gardens.

**Q: What is the difference between treated and untreated bulbs?**

A: Treated bulbs are also known as forced bulbs, which means that commercial bulb growers expose bulbs to a cold temperature to force them into flower earlier. Many spring-flowering bulbs like tulips, daffodils and hyacinths are native to the northern hemisphere, where winters are cold. In warmer climates these bulbs are artificially temperature-treated to force the rapid development of flower embryos inside the bulbs so that they will be in flower within three months instead of five months, as with untreated bulbs. Treated bulbs will all flower uniformly, earlier than normal, last longer and grow taller. Treated bulbs have to be planted as soon as possible, within 10 days at most after treatment, to ensure success.

**Q: I planted daffodil bulbs, which never produced any flowers. I want to plant daffodils again and would like to know what needs to be done to ensure a floral display.**

A: There may be several factors responsible for daffodils not flowering:

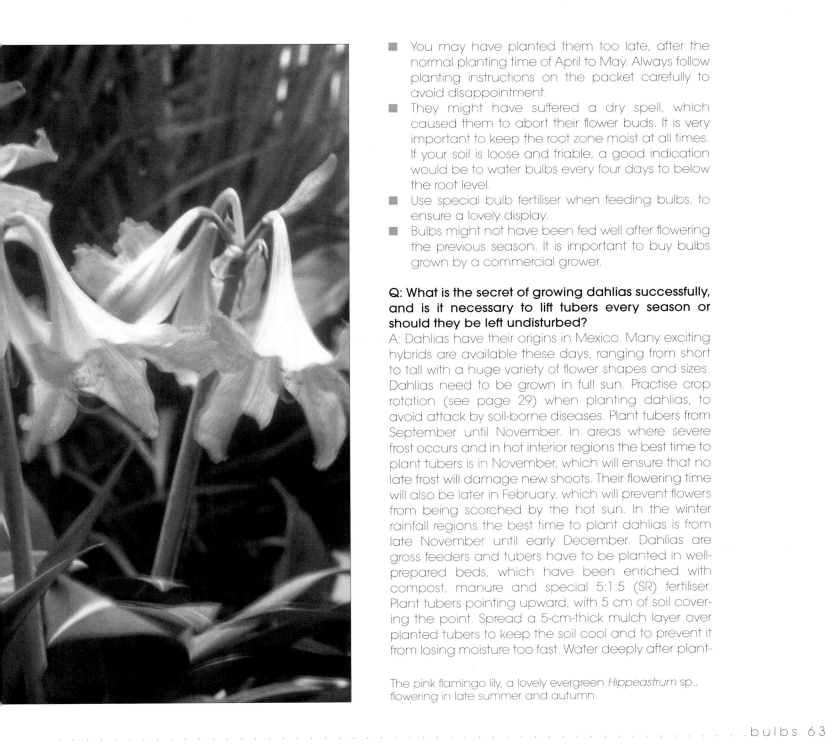

- You may have planted them too late, after the normal planting time of April to May. Always follow planting instructions on the packet carefully to avoid disappointment.
- They might have suffered a dry spell, which caused them to abort their flower buds. It is very important to keep the root zone moist at all times. If your soil is loose and friable, a good indication would be to water bulbs every four days to below the root level.
- Use special bulb fertiliser when feeding bulbs, to ensure a lovely display.
- Bulbs might not have been fed well after flowering the previous season. It is important to buy bulbs grown by a commercial grower.

**Q: What is the secret of growing dahlias successfully, and is it necessary to lift tubers every season or should they be left undisturbed?**

A: Dahlias have their origins in Mexico. Many exciting hybrids are available these days, ranging from short to tall with a huge variety of flower shapes and sizes. Dahlias need to be grown in full sun. Practise crop rotation (see page 29) when planting dahlias, to avoid attack by soil-borne diseases. Plant tubers from September until November. In areas where severe frost occurs and in hot interior regions the best time to plant tubers is in November, which will ensure that no late frost will damage new shoots. Their flowering time will also be later in February, which will prevent flowers from being scorched by the hot sun. In the winter rainfall regions the best time to plant dahlias is from late November until early December. Dahlias are gross feeders and tubers have to be planted in well-prepared beds, which have been enriched with compost, manure and special 5:1:5 (SR) fertiliser. Plant tubers pointing upward, with 5 cm of soil covering the point. Spread a 5-cm-thick mulch layer over planted tubers to keep the soil cool and to prevent it from losing moisture too fast. Water deeply after plant-

The pink flamingo lily, a lovely evergreen *Hippeastrum* sp., flowering in late summer and autumn.

ing and keep the soil moist at root level at all times. Always water in the morning to avoid plants being wet during the night, which will help to reduce the risk of mildew. Use a foliar feed throughout the growing season at monthly intervals. Tall-growing varieties will need to be staked. Cut blooms early in the morning for them to last well in the vase. Dahlia tubers should be lifted in areas that suffer severe frost, in winter rainfall regions and in subtropical areas during May. Store them in boxes in a dry place, with the tubers covered with dry soil or river sand.

## Q: What is the best way to grow the pineapple flower?

A: The pineapple flower or pineapple lily (*Eucomis autumnalis*) is an indigenous true bulb, which occurs naturally in the Eastern Cape, Northern Province, Zimbabwe and Malawi. It is a summer-flowering bulb with lovely yellow-green to purplish flowers that last well in water when cut. Plant bulbs in spring in well-drained, compost-enriched soil, with the neck of the bulb just below the soil surface. Choose a position with morning sun and afternoon shade. Bulbs can stay undisturbed in the soil during winter. They are very easy to propagate by means of seeds, which are available from the national botanical society.

## Q: How should we go about growing bulbs in glass bowls filled with water?

A: This method of growing bulbs in water is called hydroponics. The best bulbs to grow by this method are hyacinths, paperwhite narcissi and cold-treated bulbs. The secret is to keep the water level at the base of the bulb constant at all times. The most attractive containers are clear glass bowls or vases. Use washed gravel or glass balls in the container so that roots can grow through them to anchor the plant. Always use clear water only. It is not necessary to add fertiliser.

## Q: I was given a Eucharis lily a few years ago, but I do not seem to be able to get these bulbs to flower again. What are their requirements?

A: The Eucharis lily, also known as the Amazon or Madonna lily (*Eucharis grandiflora*), is native to the tropical forests of South America. They are not frost-hardy and are best grown in large containers in bright shade. They have to be brought indoors in areas where temperatures drop below 10 °C. The Eucharis lily multiplies quickly and can be divided during September. To induce bulbs to flower, plants need a constant day and night temperature of 27 °C for four weeks, whereafter a temperature of 21 °C must be maintained for at least 12 weeks. The soil must be barely moist during the cooler period. They also resent being watered with poor quality water. Their usual flowering period is from October to November, with a second flowering period possible during May.

## Q: Where can peonies be grown?

A: Tuberous perennial peonies will grow in areas with cold winters in a semi-shade or morning-sun position. They need compost-enriched, well-drained soil. They are gross feeders and need lots of water during their active growing season in summer, as well as regular feeding throughout the growing season. They must be left undisturbed in the soil and enjoy a thick mulch of organic material at all times. They flower from spring to early summer and die down during winter. Mark their position so that they will not be disturbed or damaged during their dormant period in winter. They can also be grown in large containers placed in a cool position.

Paperwhite narcissi are excellent to grow hydroponically in a glass bowl.

# trees, shrubs and climbers

Trees, shrubs and climbers form the background to any garden and, if well chosen, can also contribute greatly to a low-maintenance garden. They can screen unsightly views, reduce traffic noise and provide protection against winds and the sun where needed. There are many different evergreen and deciduous varieties to choose from to suit your particular climate, soil type and style. The diversity in foliage colour, shape and texture is huge, but just as important are the beauty and interest of bark and twigs and the fragrance and colour of flowers and fruit. A selection of both deciduous and evergreen species will add interest to your garden by providing contrast in size, form and colour throughout the year. Evergreens can provide lovely shade on hot summer days and deciduous varieties will let the winter sun through to warm the patio, home and otherwise shaded garden areas.

Climbers are great space-saving plants, as they grow vertically against or over a supporting structure. They can provide a lovely foliage background for garden features and plants. Some climbers, such as ivies, can be self-clinging by attaching themselves to walls and trees with aerial roots or sucker pads, while others, for example pandorea, grow by twining their stems around an available support. Some, like clematis, develop tendrils to grasp wire- or trelliswork to keep their stems upright, while scramblers, such as bougainvillea, lean on their supports. Many have beautiful flowers or autumn foliage and are ideal for hiding unsightly walls, fences or even a dead tree.

When buying plants, be sure to select the right plant for the job you want. If in any doubt, consult a trained horticulturist for expert advice. It is also a good idea to look around in your neighbourhood to see which plants do well in your area. Try to imagine the mature plant in three dimensions, as size is very important for balance; this will ensure that the plant is in scale with the house and the property. Since water conservation is becoming increasingly important, you should take advantage of the great selection of available indigenous plant material that is suited to your area and will have the added benefit of attracting birds to your garden.

## Planting

Correct planting and soil preparation are of the utmost importance, as trees, shrubs and climbers will become permanent features in the garden. Most plants these days are grown in nursery pots or black nursery bags and can be planted out into the garden throughout the year, while bare-rooted deciduous plants like roses and fruit trees are planted in winter and early spring. Most plants prefer well-drained soil. Drainage work will have to be done beforehand on waterlogged soil; heavy clay soil will need

A good selection of trees, shrubs and climbers of both deciduous and evergreen species will add interest to your garden by providing contrast in size, form and colour.

a lot of organic material and coarse river sand worked into it, while sandy soils will improve with lots of organic matter worked into it. Water plants in containers well before planting out, so that the root ball is moist when planting out.

1. Dig a square hole approximately two to three times wider and deeper than the container of the plant, usually 60 cm x 60 cm x 60 cm.
2. Keep the soil from the top half of the hole on one side and the soil from the bottom of the hole on the other side. Soil from the top half is much more fertile than that from deeper down.
3. Break up the soil in the bottom of the hole to loosen it.
4. Replace the soil from the top half so that it will be close to the roots. Add a cupful of superphosphate or bone meal as well as two to three spadefuls of organic material (compost) and mix with the soil from the top half in the hole.
5. Mix the soil from the bottom of the hole, which is on the opposite side of the hole, with half a cup of general fertiliser like 2:3:2 (22).
6. Fill the hole with this to the required depth of the plant.
7. Carefully remove the plant from the container and place the plant in the hole so that the garden soil is at the same level as the soil in the container.
8. Fill the area around the root ball with the rest of the soil from the bottom half, mixed with general fertiliser, and firm it down. Use the leftover soil to form a raised wall in a ring around the plant to form an irrigation basin.
9. Water well and spread organic material over the surface to form a mulch. Do not place the mulch against the plant stem as it may cause fungal infection.
10. Stake the tree or shrub, if necessary, by pushing in the stake next to the root ball to avoid damage to roots. Tie the plant to the stake with expanding material like nylon stockings, using a figure-of-eight knot. Never use wire for this purpose as it will cut into the stem of the plant. Water thoroughly.

Remember never to let roots come into direct contact with any fertiliser, as this can cause root burn. Always mix fertiliser well with soil so that it will be well distributed throughout the hole.

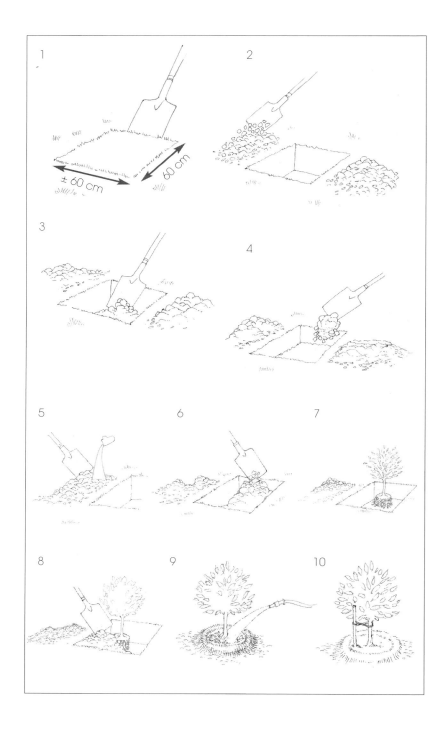

## Maintenance

All trees, shrubs and climbers will need to be fed throughout the growing season to maintain healthy growth. It is a good idea to keep plants mulched to help keep the soil damp and to prevent weeds from growing.

Start feeding established plants in spring with 3:1:5 (26) SR (for flowering plants) or 2:3:2 (22) (for non-flowering plants) at a rate of 60 g/m², spread evenly over the drip area of the plant. Repeat every two months in the active growing season. Never put fertiliser on dry soil without watering it in afterwards, as chemical burn can occur with fertilisers that have no slow-release properties.

Many trees, shrubs or climbers need occasional pruning or trimming. Most plants, however, are self-shaping so that pruning will rarely be necessary; but remember always to remove any green parts from variegated-foliage shrubs when they appear, in order to prevent the plant from reverting completely to its original green form. For pruning, see the next chapter.

## Transplanting established trees or shrubs

Smaller trees and shrubs can be transplanted successfully – if done correctly – during their dormant period. Not all plants transplant readily; deciduous species and plants with fibrous root systems like azaleas, camellias, gardenias, conifers and citrus are easier to transplant successfully.

Deciduous species should be transplanted during winter when they are leafless, while evergreen species should be transplanted during early autumn and subtropical plants during early spring.

1. The first step in transplanting a tree or shrub would be to prune the roots of the plant in early spring. This is done to promote more fibrous root growth. Do this by forcing a sharp spade into the soil at a slight angle to a depth of about 25 cm, moving in a circle with a radius of about 30 cm around the stem (for medium-sized plants). This may vary for different-sized plants.
2. Water and fertilise the plant after root pruning. Root-pruned evergreens are usually transplanted the following autumn and deciduous plants the following winter.

*Rhododendron indicum* 'Rose Queen' (formerly *Azalea indica*) is a prolific bloomer.

3. Prepare a hole – made large enough – with lots of organic material. Do not add chemical fertiliser at this stage.
4. It is a good idea to spray evergreen plants with a chemical solution like Vapor Guard or Wilt-Pruf to prevent transpiration, so that the plant will not wilt and lose too much moisture through its leaves.
5. Before plants are dug out, make sure that the soil is moist before starting to dig. It will make digging easier and the soil will cling better around the root ball.
6. Remove lower branches to make digging easier and tie up other branches where necessary. Mark the east-facing side, so that it can be planted facing the same direction again. This will help to reduce transplant stress.
7. With the stem of the plant as the middle of a circle with a diameter of about 50 cm (for a medium-sized plant), dig a trench 30 to 40 cm wide in a circle around the plant. The radius and the depth of the root ball will depend on the size of the plant and its root system. One will have to estimate when to start undercutting the root ball in order to cut off the last remaining roots at its bottom, to separate it from the surrounding soil.
8. To lift the plant out of the hole, a piece of strong material like hessian or canvas is needed. Roll up the material tightly to halfway and place the rolled-up part against the root ball. Lift or manoeuvre the root ball over the rolled-up part of the material and unroll so that the root ball will lie in the middle of the material.
9. By grabbing opposite corners of the material two or more people will be able to lift the plant out of the hole. Take care that the root ball remains intact. If it has to be transported for some distance, the root ball will have to be tied up with the material to prevent the soil from falling off.
10. Top growth of the plant will now have to be reduced by the same amount as that of root loss. If, for example, an estimated 40% of roots were lost one will have to prune the plant so that 40% leaves with branches are removed.
11. The plant can now be planted in the prepared hole, facing in the same direction as in its previous position, and then watered, mulched and staked.
12. The plant needs to be watered until it is established. The soil should be kept moist but not soggy.

## Questions and answers

### Q: I have been given a bonsai tree. How do I take care of it?

A: Most bonsai trees are miniaturised trees or shrubs and will need as much light as possible, with some direct sunlight. The best place for it would be a north-facing patio or veranda with some dappled shade in the afternoon. The soil in the container dries out very quickly and needs to be watered once and sometimes twice a day in hot and dry weather. When watering, try to drench the foliage as well. It is necessary to feed your bonsai once a month during the active growing season with diluted pot plant food. You will have to trim your bonsai constantly in order to retain its shape. Repot your bonsai only when new growth is very slow; this needs to be done in early spring. When repotting, remember to prune the roots and to remove the same amount of top growth as was removed from the roots. Use a well-draining potting mix that is also moisture-retentive, or make your own by mixing two parts of good garden loam soil with two parts compost or peat moss and one part river sand. Do not add any fertiliser at this stage; start feeding your repotted bonsai only once it is established.

Well-chosen trees, shrubs and a climber, Virginia creeper (*Parthenocissus quinquefolia*), contribute greatly to blending the house with the garden.

**Q: Some years ago we planted a wisteria, which has grown to cover the pergola completely but is not flowering very well. Does it need pruning, or is there something else we can do to make it flower better?**

A: You can prune your wisteria by cutting the long shoots back to the fifth bud from the main stem in winter. Feed with 500 g superphosphate or bone meal by spreading it out over the root area on moist soil. Cultivate lightly and water well. Cover the roots with mulch at all times. Water well in early spring during dry weather. Wisteria plants need cold winters to induce flower buds to set. Perhaps your garden is not cold enough to promote an abundance of flowers.

**Q: Could you list some climbers that will cling to a wall, as well as others that can be trained on a trellis?**

A: **Climbers that will cling to a wall are:** *Campsis grandiflora* (Chinese trumpet-creeper), *Campsis radicans* (Chinese trumpet), *Distictis laxiflora*, *Ficus pumila* (tickey creeper), *Hedera helix* (ivy), *Parthenocissus quinquefolia* (Virginia creeper) and *P. tricuspidata* (Boston ivy).

**Climbers suitable for a trellis are:** clematis, *Clerodendrum splendens* (scarlet clerodendrum), *Gelsemium sempervirens* (Carolina jasmine), *Mandevilla amoena* 'Alice du Pont' (pink dipladenia), *Mandevilla boliviensis* (white dipladenia), *Pandorea jasminoides* (bower plant), *Stephanotis floribunda* (Madagascar jasmine), *Trachelospermum jasminoides* (star jasmine).

**Q: I would like to grow a creeper against a wall of my house. The wall has to be painted every few years. What is the best method of attaching a creeper to the wall?**

A: The best method would be to fix a wooden trellis or stiff metal mesh to the wall, spacing it about 2,5 cm away from the wall. Do this by attaching wooden spacers so that the trellis can be fixed in such a way that it is hinged at the bottom edge, which will allow the creeper to be eased away from the wall for painting.

**Q: We have recently moved into a property with three large rubber trees. I am told that these trees are liable to damage the foundations of the house. If these trees were to be cut down, would they grow out again and if so, how can the stumps be killed?**

A: Rubber trees have a very invasive root system and should be taken out. Stumps will most probably grow out again and will have to be killed with a tree killer like Garlon 4 (follow recommended rates carefully), or the stumps will have to be dug out if you want to plant some other trees in the same position. If the stumps are left in the ground and are dead, you can speed up the rotting process by keeping them moist and watering them with a solution of ammonium sulphate at a rate of two tablespoons per 10 litres of water every 14 days. This, however, is quite a time-consuming process and it may take years before the stumps are completely rotted away.

**Q: We experience some light frost during winter. Which palms can we plant around our pool area?**

A: Plant palms at least 4 metres away from the pool. Choose from the following: *Bismarckia nobilis*, *Butia capitata* (jelly palm), *Chamaerops humilis* (European fan palm), *\*Phoenix reclinata* (wild date palm), *Seaforthia elegans* (solitaire palm) or *Archontophoenix cunninghamiana* (king or piccabeen palm), *Syagrus romanzoffiana* or *Cocos plumosa* (queen palm), *Trachycarpus fortunei* (Chinese windmill palm), *Washingtonia filifera* (petticoat palm), *Washingtonia robusta* (green-leaved petticoat palm).

Evergreen conifers are an excellent choice for low-maintenance gardening. Here *Thuja orientalis* 'Golden Rocket' softens the perimeter wall in a formal planting with a laurel (*Prunus laurocerasus*) hedge in the middle and *Syzugium paniculatum* at the bottom.

*Encephalartos transvenosus* (Modjaji cycad) adds a tropical feel to the garden.

**Q: Which are the best trees to plant in the lawn? Could you list some that are not messy so that we will not have to rake up the leaves in autumn?**
A: *Acacia burkei* (black monkey thorn), *A. caffra* (common hook thorn), *A. galpinii* (monkey thorn), *A. karroo* (sweet thorn), *A. pendula* (weeping myall), *Agonis flexuosa* (willow myrtle), *Albizia julibrissin* (silk tree), *Caesalpinia ferrea* (leopard tree), *Ceratonia siliqua* (carob), *Cinnamomum camphora* (camphor tree), *Cussonia paniculata* (mountain cabbage tree), *C. spicata* (common cabbage tree), *Diospyros whyteana* (bladdernut), *Eucalyptus ficifolia* (red flowering gum), *Harpephyllum caffrum* (wild plum), *Hymenosporum flavum* (sweetshade), *Ilex mitis* (Cape holly), *Loxostylis alata* (tarwood), *Magnolia grandiflora* (laurel magnolia), *Melaleuca linariifolia* (flax-leaved myrtle), *Millettia grandis* (umzimbeet), *Olea europaea* subsp. *africana* (wild olive), *Ptaeroxylon obliquum* (sneezewood), *Quercus ilex* (holly oak), *Rhus lancea* (karree), *R. leptodictya* (mountain karree), *R. pendulina* (white karree), *Stenocarpus sinuatus* (Queensland fire-wheel tree).

**Q: Why does my English holly tree have no berries?**
A: Your holly tree is probably a male plant. Only trees with female flowers will bear fruit if pollen from a male tree is available.

**Q: Why does one have to cut back trees and shrubs when they are transplanted?**
A: When transplanting a plant the root system gets disturbed, and by reducing the size of the plant's total leaf surface area, i.e. the area exposed to the drying effects of wind and sun, the remaining roots can support the plant more easily.

**Q: When is the best time to transplant cycads?**
A: The best time would be in August before new growth starts. If the plants have many fronds, you will have to reduce the amount by half.

**Q: When is the best time to prune flowering shrubs?**
A: Many shrubs flower on the previous year's and older wood, and these shrubs should be pruned or cut back in spring immediately after flowering. Shrubs that flower on shoots of the current season can be pruned in late winter before new growth starts.

**Q: Where is the best place to grow roses?**
A: Roses will grow in most well-drained, slightly acid soils (pH 6,5 is ideal). They need at least six hours of direct sunlight, preferably morning sun, to flourish. Grow roses either in separate rosebeds or in a mixed shrub and herbaceous border. Floribunda and English-style roses, in particular, are

excellent for this purpose. Do not grow roses in the lawn in separate little islands, especially if you have a Kikuyu lawn – the competition for water and nutrients will be too fierce. There are also many varieties that will flourish in containers; ground cover-type roses and miniatures are very good for this purpose.

**Q: We recently moved into another home. I planted some roses, which look sick. I replaced these bushes with yet more, and these also look sick. Why can I no longer grow roses?**
A: The problem you are experiencing is quite common and known as replant sickness or rose soil sickness. This is caused by planting roses in the same soil where old roses were growing previously. The old roses may have been perfectly healthy, but they prevent new rose plants from establishing themselves. You have three options for coping with this problem. The first is to avoid the bad bed and establish roses in a completely new area. The second is to replace the soil by digging holes of at least 60 cm x 60 cm and deep-filling these holes with fresh soil. The third option is to let the soil lie fallow for a few years or to grow different kinds of plants not related to the rose family in that area.

**Q: Could you please recommend some highly scented hybrid tea and floribunda roses?**
A: **Hybrid teas:** Alec's Red, Ambassador, Apricot Silk, Avon, Bewitched, Big Purple, Blue Moon, Bushveld Dawn, Crysler Imperial, Double Delight, Duftwolke, Ecstasy, Flamingo, Garden Perfume, Granada, Harmonie, Just Joey, Koningin Beatrix, Lady Like, Memoire, Mister Lincoln, New Zealand, Oklahoma, Red 'n Fragrant, Sheila's Perfume, Spiced Coffee, St. John's College, Summer Lady, Tanned Beauty.
**Floribunda roses:** Bella Rosa, Colchester Beauty, Courvoisier, Elizabeth of Glamis, Majolika, Manou Meilland, Margaret Merril.
**David Austin's English roses are also highly recommended. For scented roses, plant:** Abraham Darby, Ambridge Rose, Charlotte, Cottage Rose, Eglantyne, Gertrude Jekyll, Glamis Castle, Golden Celebration, Graham Thomas, Jude the Obscure, L.D. Braithwaite, Margaret Roberts, Mary Rose, Molineaux, Noble Antony, Pat Austin, Perdita, Scepter'd Isle, Sharifa Asma, Sophy's Rose, The Dark Lady, The Prince, Tradescant, Winchester Cathedral.

**Q: Is it necessary to prune a yellow banksia rose?**
A: No. Banksia roses are not pruned as such, as these roses bear their flowers on the old wood. You can, however, trim and shape the plant in spring immediately after flowering.

'L.D. Braithwaite', a free-flowering variety with a light Old Rose fragrance.

**Q: How does one recognise suckers on a rose bush and is it necessary to remove them?**
A: Roses are grafted or budded on a rootstock. Suckers are shoots that arise from below the bud union and the foliage will differ from that of the good rose. They have to be removed as soon as they appear.

**Q: Can you give me some advice on how to grow hibiscus successfully?**
A: Hibiscus are tropical plants and flourish in warm, humid areas. They are quite adaptable, however, and will grow in areas where light frost occurs if plants are grown in a sheltered position or protected from frost during winter. Hibiscus bear flowers on new shoots and therefore should be pruned in early spring, once the danger of late frost is past. They require well-drained, humus-enriched soil and should be fertilised in spring, mid-summer and autumn with a general fertiliser high in potash (K), for example 3:1:5 (26), at a rate of 60 g/m². Water well during dry weather and keep the plants mulched.

**Q: Could you list some shrubs that would be ideal for cut-flower and/or cut-foliage purposes?**
A: **For foliage:** *Abelia chinensis*, *Abelia* 'Edward Goucher', *Abelia* 'Francis Mason', camellias, *Coprosma repens* (mirror plant), *Elaeagnus pungens* 'Maculata' (thorny oleaster), *\*Elegia capensis* (broom reed), *Ligustrum lucidum* grafted varieties (privet), *Melaleuca* spp., *Murraya exotica* (orange jessamine), *Nandina domestica* (sacred bamboo), *Pittosporum* spp., *Phormium* spp. (flax), *Prunus cerasifera* 'Nigra' (purple cherry plum), *Ruscus aculeatus* (butcher's broom), *Sarcococca confusa* (Christmas box), *\*Strelitzia* spp. (crane flowers).
**For flowers:** azaleas, camellias, *Chaenomeles speciosa* (Japanese flowering quince), *Chamaelaucium uncinatum* (Geraldton waxplant), *Hydrangea macrophylla* varieties, *Hydrangea quercifolia* (oak-leaf hydrangea), lavenders, *Leptospermum scoparium* (tea bush), *\*Leucadendron* spp. (conebushes), *\*Leucospermum* spp. (pincushion proteas), *Pentas lanceolata*, *\*Plumbago* spp., *\*Protea* spp., *Raphiolepis* spp. (hawthorns), roses, *Strelitzia* spp. (crane flowers).
**For berries and seeds:** *\*Asclepias fruticosa* (milkweed), *Cotoneaster* varieties.

**Q: What is the best way to safeguard conifers against attack from the cypress aphid?**
A: The Italian cypress aphid feeds by sucking sap from conifer twigs and branches during winter. They excrete a potent toxin whilst feeding, which causes foliage to turn brown. By early summer the dead branches and plants are the only signs that the aphids were there. Gardeners who want to protect their conifers from this pest will have to follow a control programme, starting in early March. The most effective way of control is to use a systemic aphicide. A systemic insecticide enters the plant either through its leaves or through the roots and makes the plant sap poisonous to sucking insects. Beneficial insects like ladybirds, bees, wasps and spiders are not affected by this poison. Use Efekto Insecticide Granules by sprinkling one tablespoon per m² and watering well to soak the root area thoroughly, or use a solution of Metasystox at a rate of 10 ml to 10 litres of water and drench the root area (1 m²). Conifers smaller than 2 m can be sprayed with a solution of Metasystox, Dursban E or Aphicide. You will have to spray throughout autumn and winter, starting in March. Treat every two weeks during March and April and thereafter once a month until spring.

Pink 'Flower Carpet' roses are excellent in the garden, as ground cover or in containers.

# pruning

Pruning is one of the most creative aspects of gardening. Through this process we can control the size and shape of plants and, consequently, their flowers and fruits. Essentially, pruning is manipulating the hormones of plants, which influences the way the plant will grow. By removing some buds through pruning we force others to grow.

Most trees and shrubs are self-shaping and need to be pruned only rarely, while others are greatly improved by regular or occasional pruning. Through pruning we can achieve the following goals:

- To shape a plant as it grows, especially when it is young. We can make it shorter or bushier and ensure a balanced framework. With a hedge, for example, our aim is to promote dense growth from the bottom upwards.
- To rejuvenate an old and leggy plant. By eliminating old growth we can stimulate new shoots to take over. When we remove spent flowers from shrubs, for example, we prevent the plant from forming fruits and seeds and so redirect the plant's energy to further flowering and vegetative growth.
- To eliminate competition with other plants and between branches for light, by reducing the overall size and by thinning out branches.
- To remove dead and diseased wood or unwanted branches that have reverted from a variegated form to a green form, for example, or to remove suckers from a rootstock on certain grafted plants.
- To remove spindly and poorly developed wood. The plant will only waste energy in trying to keep these weak growths alive. By removing them the plant can channel this energy into stronger and more productive wood.
- To train plants in novel forms, such as topiary work where sculptural shapes are achieved, or to train certain plants in a two-dimensional pattern with the espalier technique.

Pruning on selected deciduous plants is usually done in winter and early spring, when they are still dormant. Evergreens, however, do not need to be pruned like deciduous trees; they usually only need shaping. Any dead, diseased or damaged wood should be removed as soon as it is noticed. This can be done any time of the year. Generally, most spring-flowering shrubs and some flowering trees that flower on the previous season's wood are pruned after they have flowered. The best time is when the petals have dropped but before too much new shoot growth has taken place. Shrubs that flower on the current season's growth (on new wood) in summer and autumn, are pruned in winter. Most bushy shrubs require little pruning. They only need some rejuvenating every three or four years: by removing some older branches at ground level new growth will be promoted. Remember the general rule: the more severely you prune a plant, the more vigorous the regrowth will be.

Clipped boxwood (*Buxus sempervirens*) hedges in geometric patterns form the basic design element of this formal walled garden. The obelisks are planted with climbing Iceberg roses.

## Pruning methods

Pruning tools like secateurs, pruning saws, shears and long-handled loppers must always be sharp and clean to ensure clean cuts at all times. Bruised and jagged cuts will only cause the plant to heal more slowly and provide a breeding place for disease. Large cuts can be sealed with a sealant that contains a fungicide; it is not necessary to seal cuts smaller than 1 cm in diameter.

- Pruning by means of the standard pruning procedure. This is usually done with pruning secateurs or loppers. The cut must always be made close to a bud at a slight angle. Removing thicker and heavier branches will have to be done in stages with a saw to prevent branches from breaking and tearing. Trim back branches up to about 40 cm long, which can then easily be removed cleanly.
- Clipping or shearing is usually done with hedge shears to promote denser and sturdier growth. The entire outer shape of the plant is clipped with shears. This method is usually applied to hedges every two months during summer.
- Thinning is done with secateurs, loppers or a saw to open up a plant. Old wood and competing branches crossing one another can be removed by this method. Thinning is usually done at the same time as cut-pruning.
- Pinching is the removal of the terminal bud of a shoot by hand. This is usually done to young plants and seedlings to promote bushier growth, and can be done throughout the year.

## The pruning of roses

We prune roses to encourage the plant to produce better blooms and to keep it young and vigorous. It is not difficult to prune roses if you go about it with common sense. With careful observation you will quickly learn to recognise old or diseased wood that needs to be removed. Prune your roses in winter. In very cold areas, where there is danger of late frost, prune roses in mid- to late August. In warmer regions, where roses don't lose all their foliage, prune in mid- to late July.

The following basic principles apply to the pruning of all hybrid tea and floribunda roses. Note, however, that 'Iceberg' floribunda roses should not be pruned too hard.

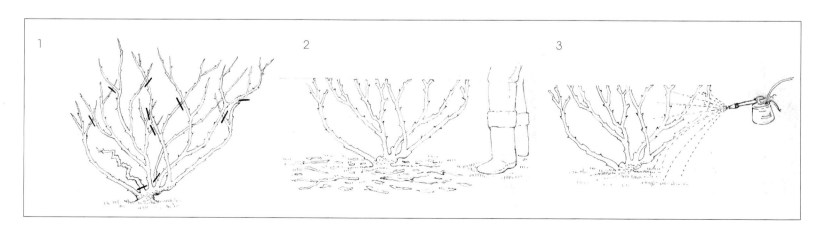

1. First cut out all dead and diseased wood. Remove all spindly and twiggy growth thinner than a pencil. Remember never to leave a stump when cutting out canes, as the leftover stump may die back into the main stem or bud union and cause disease to enter. Take a careful look at the bush and thin out branches crossing or rubbing against one another. Always take out the older wood so that the younger, more vigorous shoots can develop further.
2. The remaining canes can now be shortened by about one-third. Medium-sized bushes will have canes up to knee height left over after pruning. It is not necessary always to make the cut at an outward-facing bud: rather choose the most promising bud (well developed and fat). It is preferable, however, that the bud should face in an outward direction, as it will influence the shape of the bush. In winter rainfall regions and areas of high humidity, cuts can be sealed with a specific sealant containing a fungicide. Do not use ordinary paint.
3. Clean up all leaves and cut-off pieces and destroy them. Spray bushes and surrounding soil with lime sulphur at a rate of one part lime sulphur to ten parts of water (winter strength). Remember to use fresh lime sulphur every year, as it does not keep well over long periods of time. Repeat the application after 14 days. Be careful not to spray new shoots with lime sulphur, as it will burn the new growth.

## Pruning different types of roses

- New rose bushes usually need drastic pruning to promote new growth. Cut canes back to about 17 cm long. Always try to keep three to four well-spaced canes and an open centre.
- Climbing roses are not pruned for at least the first three years. Let the climber become established first and let the vertical canes grow up to 3 m tall. They can then be tied onto horizontal supports in a fan shape, spacing them evenly apart on both sides from the middle. When pruning, first remove old and unproductive wood. Cut back the side shoots on the main canes to about three buds. Shorten the main canes by a third if they are getting too long for the support structure. Note: Do not prune yellow and white banksia roses; they only need some thinning and shaping when necessary.
- Standard roses are pruned the same way as for hybrid tea and floribunda roses.
- Miniature roses are not pruned hard. Here it is only necessary to thin out all dead, diseased and spindly growth. The main canes can be reduced by half if bushes are getting too big. Alternatively, bushes can be trimmed with hedge shears to promote bushy growth.
- Heritage roses that only flower during spring should be pruned only after they have finished flowering (usually in November) in order to encourage new growth for the next season's flowers. Others, like the Gallicas and damasks, can be reduced to half their size by eliminating all unproductive canes.
- Ground-cover roses can be trimmed with hedge shears during mid-summer, and should be pruned like bush roses in winter.

## Fruit trees

Why should fruit trees be pruned? We prune young fruit trees to establish a strong framework of branches. Pruning stimulates new growth, which will promote flowering and more fruit. The fruit is easier to harvest if we reduce the top growth and open up the centre to allow sunlight to enter the tree. With more sunlight in the centre of the tree, fruit becomes more colourful and develops better flavour because the natural sugars are increased. The quality of fruit improves, resulting in larger fruit if we eliminate excess fruiting wood. Pruning also

The art of topiary is still popular today, with plant sculptures adorning many gardens.

maintains the tree at a height where fruit can be reached, and makes it easier and cheaper to spray smaller trees. Fruit trees take up less space in the garden if they are regularly pruned and trees also have a much tidier appearance.

Deciduous fruit trees are pruned to an open vase shape in winter. During the first few years they are usually pruned hard to shape them, whereafter the pruning becomes much lighter, entailing only the removing of dead or diseased branches or branches crossing one another, the thinning of side shoots and the cutting back of main branches. Evergreen fruit trees are not pruned, but only shaped if necessary. For pruning of fruit trees, see the next chapter.

Grapes bear fruit on new growth and, depending on the cultivar, are pruned accordingly. When planting a new grapevine, cut back to two buds or eyes after planting. For growing the vine on a trellis, allow the main shoot to develop to the desired height during summer before topping it. Remove all side shoots in the meantime. Allow two main shoots to develop from this main stem on either side to train along the trellis. A framework of canes must be built up before winter pruning can be done. Most grapes can be pruned by shortening the long lateral growths on the framework to two or three buds. Grapes are borne on the current season's growth that develops from the buds left on the pruned framework.

## Topiary

Topiary is the art of training and clipping trees and shrubs into familiar, three-dimensional ornamental shapes. Simple, geometric shapes are generally used for formal gardens. More elaborate shapes like animals, birds, etc. can be used to complement other designs.

To do topiary work, you will first have to choose an appropriate plant with many dormant buds so that new growth will start anywhere a cut is made. The plant should have small foliage or needles, must be evergreen and should grow fast. Appropriate plants for topiary work are common boxwood (*Buxus sempervirens*), bay (*Laurus nobilis*), *Cotoneaster* varieties, English holly (*Ilex aquifolium*), privet (*Ligustrum* varieties), *Thuja* species and rosemary, to name a few.

To start training a plant, you have to choose a form to train it into. Cut out any dead wood and don't choose a shape that will leave the bottom part shaded, since it tends to die. Clip your topiary form regularly to keep it full and well manicured. You can also train climbers like ivy or the tickey creeper on a preshaped aluminium- or copper-wire frame for an almost instant topiary design.

## Espaliering

Espaliers are two-dimensional, trained plants. It is an excellent way to grow mainly fruit trees in a confined space against a structure or wall as an ornament or feature. It is surprisingly easy to use this technique in training fruit trees and ornamental plants. Some plants that lend themselves very well to espaliering are grafted fruit trees like apples, pears, cherries, peaches, apricots, plums and ornamentals such as Japanese maples, magnolias, camellias, flowering quince, cotoneasters and poinsettias. There are many shapes to choose from, as long as they are two-dimensional.

The easiest is to train a plant against a series of horizontal wires spaced 30–40 cm apart against a wall or on a free-standing structure.

Remember that a north- or west-facing wall will be very hot with reflected heat and should be avoided for espaliering. Plant your tree or shrub against a support structure and leave it to grow freely for a year before starting to train it. To encourage horizontal branching, cut off the main stem to just above the third bud. When the three shoots that grow out of these buds have reached a length of about 50 cm, the two lowest ones are tied onto the horizontal wires, with the third tied vertically. This vertical branch is cut back during the next winter to just above two opposite buds near the second set of horizontal wires, and so the process goes on. The next vertical branch will be taken from the next upright bud along one of the horizontal branches.

## Questions and answers

**Q: When is the best time to prune a hedge and how should I prune it to prevent the bottom part from going bare?**
A: Most hedges need to be pruned more than once during the year. To keep hedges in good shape, start trimming in early summer after the first growth flush. A second trimming might be necessary in late summer as well. Train the hedge so that the bottom part is wider than the top. In this way the sun will reach the whole surface of the hedge. If the bottom part is shaded it will die back and become bare.

**Q: How does one raise a standard?**
A: It is very easy to raise one's own standards; it only takes patience and time. Choose any woody plant with a straight stem and stake it. Start from the bottom by removing all side shoots for up to a quarter of the length of the stem. When the main stem has reached the required height, pinch off the tips of the leader and the main side shoots. As these top shoots branch out, more growth can be removed from the main stem. Continue pinching back the top shoots until the crown is fully developed, and remove all the lower growth. Keep pinching back shoots to maintain a bushy crown. *Ficus microcarpa* (ornamental fig) and *Syzygium paniculatum* (Australian brush cherry) are the most commonly used plants for this purpose in South Africa.

Shrubs and climbers can be used for espaliering. Here a common large-leaved ivy (*Hedera canariensis*) is used to good effect.

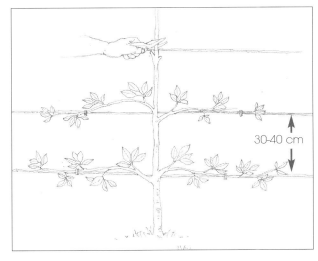

30-40 cm

**Q: What is pollarding?**
A: It is the annual pruning, virtually to the trunk, of tree branches at the desired height. The entire top can be taken off to produce a globe-like display of new shoots. It is a convenient way to keep street trees within bounds. Pollarding is generally used on poplars, willows, beeches and London planes.

**Q: Is it necessary to buy loppers for pruning roses?**
A: Loppers with their long handles provide the greater leverage required for cutting thicker wood (usually thicker than 2 cm in diameter) and enable you to reach into thorny, difficult-to-reach places in large rose bushes. A pair of loppers is definitely a must for pruning roses.

**Q: How should I prune my hydrangeas?**
A: Hydrangeas should be pruned in winter. Cut back all shoots that were flowering to within three buds from the ground. Those shoots that didn't flower should not be cut back at all. Cut out all dead, spindly and diseased wood.

**Q: I have many roses and fruit trees in my garden. Which types of secateurs are the best for long-lasting performance?**
A: There are two basic types of secateurs. The parrot-bill secateurs, which cut like scissors, should be used with the larger cutting blade nearest to the stem of the plant to be effective. They can cut side shoots flush with the main stem and fit into narrow spaces. Anvil secateurs, which chop like a knife, have the advantage of needing less applied strength to cut through stems. There is a wide variety of secateurs available, with slight variations in their design. Always buy a reputable brand with tempered blades and make sure that they fit your hand. Keep blades clean and regularly oiled.

**Q: We have a tree with the centre broken off. Will it grow into a tree or should we replace it?**
A: If there is a strong shoot near the break, it could be trained to take the place of the broken leader. Stake the plant and tie it securely below the break, then tie the chosen side shoot higher up onto the stake to train it as the new leader.

**Q: Which indigenous shrubs can I grow to train in the espalier way?**
A: Some indigenous shrubs suitable for espaliering would be: *Bauhinia galpinii* (pride of De Kaap), *Carissa bispinosa* (forest num-num), *Gardenia* spp., *Grewia occidentalis* (cross-berry), *Mackaya bella* (river bells or forest bell bush), *Ochna serrulata* (plane bush), *Polygala myrtifolia* (September bush or wild violet), *Rhamnus prinoides* (dogwood), *Rothmannia globosa* (bell gardenia) and *Tecomaria capensis* (Cape honeysuckle).

**Q: How does one prune an overgrown bougainvillea?**
A: You will have to cut back the long shoots to about the fifth bud from the base at the main stem. Trim out all twiggy growth. As soon as they start growing again you will have to train them, otherwise you will soon have them growing wild again. Bougainvilleas are usually not pruned very hard as it only encourages strong shoots to develop. They flower on older wood.

**Q: Should I prune my clematis vine?**
A: It depends on your specific clematis variety. The 'Lanuginosa', 'Jackmanii' and 'Viticella' groups should be pruned back hard to about 15 cm from the base of the last year's growth. The 'Florida', 'Patens' and 'Montana'

Topiary, hedges and an espalier form an interesting corner feature in this townhouse garden.

groups are not really pruned, but only need occasional thinning after flowering. Some strong growth can be cut back, however, if low branching is needed.

### Q: When is the best time to prune fuchsias?
A: Fuchsias should be pruned in August. Avoid pruning them too early in winter as the foliage helps insulate the plant from the cold. Once danger of frost has passed they can be pruned back by about two-thirds. Always remove dead, weak or broken stems to ensure a healthy framework from which new shoots can develop. In warmer, frost-free areas, prune back in late autumn – May is usually the best month.

# fruit, vegetables and herbs

## Fruit

No home garden can be complete without at least one fruit tree. Fruit trees and fruit-bearing plants are not difficult to grow; even on quite a small plot, space can be found for them. Citrus trees do not need a lot of space and many others can be grown along a fence, over a trellis or along the sides of buildings. There are limiting factors for gardeners, however. The climate must be taken into consideration when planting fruit trees. Always select those suited to your area and buy from a reliable nursery to avoid disappointment. Deciduous fruit trees require a certain period of cold weather to break their dormancy. In areas where the temperature does not drop low enough, buds, for example those of peaches, remain dormant in spring. They also need very careful pruning and pest and disease control. However, there are many fruit-bearing plants that do not need much attention in the way of pruning and spraying, for example figs, strawberries and passion fruit. Others need to be pollinated by another variety to bear well, like apples, pears, pecan nuts and almonds, while some are self-pollinating, such as mangoes and peaches.

Fruit trees are either deciduous (lose their leaves in winter) or evergreen, and most require a sunny position. Fruit trees for regions with cold, frosty winters and temperate summers are: apples, pears, quinces, peaches, plums, apricots, cherries and nectarines. Those for warmer areas with light frost are: almonds, avocados, kiwi fruit, oranges, grapes, figs, pecan nuts, passion fruit, persimmons and olives. For subtropical and tropical areas, suitable fruit varieties are: bananas, mangoes, litchis, pawpaw, pineapples, citrus and most of the fruit trees that grow in areas with light frost.

Fruit trees grown in containers like black nursery bags – mostly evergreen varieties – can be planted at any time of the year. Deciduous fruit trees are usually bare-root trees (from the open ground) and need to be planted in late winter, before the middle of August.

## Planting fruit trees

Fruit trees will grow in most soil types if good drainage is available. It is a good idea to prepare the holes in advance to give the soil time to settle. Dig a hole of 75 cm x 75 cm and keep the soil from the top on one side and the soil from the bottom of the hole on the other side. Break up the soil in the bottom of the hole and return

Every home garden should have a lemon tree, which is both useful and ornamental.

the topsoil, mixed with two cupfuls of superphosphate or bone meal. Mix the bottom soil with compost and fill up the hole. Mark the middle of the hole and water well to settle the soil.

To plant trees out of containers (usually a plastic nursery bag), water the plant well and open up the hole slightly larger than the size of the container. Remove the plastic bag by cutting the bottom of the bag away, place the plant in the prepared hole and slip the bag up and off. Fill the space around the root ball with soil, firm down and make a shallow basin. Mulch and water well. Make sure the tree is planted at the same depth as it was in the container.

Bare-rooted trees are planted the same way. Be sure to fill the areas around the roots well with soil and firm down. Plant these trees with their bud union about 12 cm above the soil. All newly planted trees should be staked. Insert a sturdy stake next to the tree and secure it to the tree with expanding tying material, using a figure-of-eight tie.

## Aftercare

Deciduous trees should be cut back to knee height (0,45 m) to ensure that they will develop a good shape, if they have not been preshaped in the nursery.

Water young trees once the top 3 cm of the soil is dry, until established. Thereafter they should be watered regularly every two weeks in hot and dry weather throughout the year. Always water deeply rather than giving more frequent, shallow waterings, which will only encourage roots to develop close to the soil surface.

Most fruit trees should be fertilised, starting in spring. Spread fertiliser like Wonder Flowers, Fruit and Shrubs 3:1:5 (26) SR evenly over the drip area of the tree at a rate of 100 g/m², working it into the top layer of the soil before watering. Repeat this every two months during the active growing season. Keep the soil around the trees mulched throughout the year.

Pests and diseases differ on different types of fruit trees and must be dealt with when they occur. Deciduous fruit trees and vines must be sprayed with lime sulphur (1:10 solution), which acts as both an insecticide and a fungicide, in winter while they are dormant.

## Pruning of fruit trees

The pruning of fruit trees helps create vigorous growth and encourages better quality crops.

Evergreen fruit trees are not pruned; they may only need occasional trimming and shaping. Deciduous fruit trees, if not trained into espalier form, are usually shaped to form an open cup shape.

Pome fruits, such as apples and pears, are shaped when they are planted. Three or four branches that are evenly spaced round the trunk are chosen to form the framework of the tree, and side shoots are trimmed. These trees bear their fruit on the same spurs every year and don't need pruning once the framework has been established. A little thinning can be done every winter to retain the open cup shape.

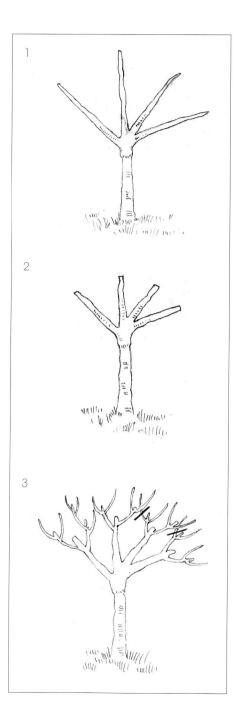

1

2

3

Stone fruits like peaches, nectarines, apricots and plums need to be pruned or shaped more severely than pome fruits every winter. These trees are shaped when planted. The object is to have an open cup-shaped tree, with three to four branches spaced evenly around the main trunk to allow sunlight and air flow for all branches.

1. Choose three or four main scaffold limbs above the bud union on the main stem from the ground. Try to prevent 'forks' forming, as these may split under the weight of the fruit.
2. On these scaffold limbs, select lateral shoots to develop as leaders. Never tip these main framework branches, as this will only stimulate growth. Try to give each branch its space in which to grow and bear fruit.
3. All side shoots growing from these scaffold limbs are selected to form a herringbone pattern. Remove all those growing inwards or crossing with main framework branches.

When trimming back the side branches of peach trees, care should be taken not to remove all the flower buds, as some varieties bear flower buds toward the tips of these side shoots. Leaf buds are single or appear in a group with flower buds. Flower buds can be distinguished from leaf buds in that they are much plumper and grouped together as either two or three buds. Any shoots below the bud union must be removed, as these can hinder the growth of the main branches. Central shoots threatening to cause congestion in the middle are removed, as well as those too near the ground, which would obstruct cultivation of the soil around the tree.

Apricots and plums only need a little trimming every year, once the main framework has been established. Cherries, however, are not pruned at all.

Almonds and pecan nuts, although deciduous, are not pruned except for initial shaping when planted. Macadamia nuts, citrus and subtropical fruits are evergreen and are not pruned, except for occasional trimming.

Peaches, nectarines, apricots and plums need to be thinned out when fruit has reached the size of a pea. A general rule is to leave only single fruits a handbreadth apart for peaches and nectarines, and slightly less for apricots and plums.

## Vegetables

To be able to harvest fresh vegetables from one's own garden is very rewarding. With careful planning and successive sowings and plantings one can have a continuous supply throughout the year. Surplus of seasonal crops can be frozen for later use.

When planning a vegetable garden, sun is of major importance. Vegetables grow best in full sun with rows running in a north-south direction to receive sunlight evenly throughout the day. The soil needs to be well drained, rich in organic matter and free of weeds. When preparing the beds, dig in lots of compost and manure with fertiliser like Wonder Planting and Vegetables 2:3:4 (21) at a rate of 60 g/m². Grow vegetable varieties suitable for your area and sow seeds at the right time of the year if seedlings are not bought from your local nursery.

Practise crop rotation by not planting vegetables from the same family in the same plot two years in succession. A good principle to follow would be to rotate a legume vegetable like beans or peas with a leaf and fruit vegetable like lettuce, cabbage, spinach, brinjals, tomatoes, broccoli, cauliflower, cucumbers, marrows, pumpkins or celery, followed by a root vegetable like beetroot, carrots, onions, potatoes, sweet potatoes, radishes, parsnips or turnips. There is a natural rotation between warm-season and cool-season vegetables anyway, so that crop rotation does not become too complicated.

Water regularly so that the soil is humid at all times, but not soggy. Harvest vegetables while young and tender and remove old plants as soon as the crop is finished.

# Herbs

Herbs are wonderfully versatile plants that can be used for cosmetic, culinary, flavouring and medicinal purposes.

Most herbs need well-drained soil in full sun, but others grow well in semi-shade. Some herbs are annuals, while others are biennials or perennials. Herbs, especially the annual varieties, can be grown in rows in the vegetable garden, or a special herb garden can be made as a feature. All herbs can be grown in pots, tubs or window boxes, as long as the container is large enough for the variety.

A large number of herbs can be started from seeds sown in spring or autumn in warm areas. Follow the same procedure as for starting flower seedlings (see pages 43-53). Once established, herbs need little attention apart from weeding and watering. Fresh herbs can be harvested as required, but those needed for drying have to be well grown before harvesting. Pick the herbs on a dry day and tie the stems together for hanging upside down in a warm, dry place. When completely dry, store the leaves in airtight bottles.

Annual herbs: anise, basil, borage, coriander, dill and savory.

Perennial and biennial herbs: angelica, caraway, chives, fennel, lavender, marjoram, mint, oregano, parsley, sage, tarragon and thyme.

Other plants: bay tree, garlic, lemon verbena, lemon grass and rosemary.

# Questions and answers

**Q: Why grow your own fruit if a great variety is available from the supermarket?**
A: If cultivated and handled correctly, home-grown fruit is far superior to market fruit. Market fruit is picked in a slightly immature condition for transporting and handling, and is often harvested before sugars and flavours have developed. Tree-ripened fruit tastes much better.

**Q: What type of fruit can be grown in a garden with limited space?**
A: Most berry plants like boysenberries, youngberries, raspberries, Cape gooseberries and strawberries do not require a lot of space. Boysen-, young- and raspberries grow on a trellis, as do granadillas, grapes and kiwi fruit. Remember to choose those fruits that will do well in your climatic region. Before planting, prepare a trellis. Plant two posts up to 2 m tall and stretch out stout wires between them on which to train the stems. Raspberry stems need to be tied onto wires vertically, while the others are trained along horizontal wires. This trellis can make an excellent screen to hide the rubbish bin or anything unsightly from the kitchen window. Grapevines and kiwi fruit are very good for covering a pergola in the right position. Cape gooseberries (annual) and strawberries can be grown in pots as long as enough sunlight is available. More dedicated gardeners can also consider growing apples, pears, peaches and apricots in the espalier fashion.

**Q: My plum tree bears a lot of fruit but they are very sour. What can I do to sweeten them, especially around the pips?**
A: Give the trees a dressing of potassium sulphate, evenly spread over the root area during spring at a rate of half a cup per tree, or fertilise with 3:1:5 (26) SR at a rate of 100 g/m$^2$, spread evenly over the drip area in spring.

An interesting vegetable garden designed on a square with pathways for access. Each corner of the square is planted differently.

## Q: Which nut trees can be grown in South Africa, and in what regions?

A: Pecan nuts (*Carya illinoinensis*) resemble walnuts in appearance and flavour. Walnuts generally do not grow well in our climate. Pecans are deciduous and will grow well in all the frost-free and temperate regions of the country. These trees grow to a very large size and are only suitable for large gardens. They require deep, well-drained soil and ample water from spring to autumn. Grow different varieties together for cross-pollination. Well-known varieties are 'Barton', 'Choctaw', 'Ukalinga' and 'Wichita', to name a few.

Macadamia or Queensland nut trees (*Macadamia ternifolia*) are evergreen and will only grow in warm, humid and frost-free areas. They grow up to 8 m tall and nuts mature during autumn and winter.

Almonds (*Prunus communis*) are deciduous and similar to peach trees. They will only bear in the more temperate regions where there is no danger of late frost and where the summers are dry. More than one tree is necessary for cross-pollination. Available varieties include 'Brits', 'Ferranges', Non Pareil', 'Peerless' and 'Texas Mission'.

## Q: When is the best time to plant strawberries?

A: Strawberries need a sunny, well-drained position and are quite adaptable to climatic regions. Strawberries should be renewed every two years to maintain a high yield. They are gross feeders and the soil must be well prepared with lots of compost, kraal manure and general fertiliser like Wonder Planting and Vegetables 2:3:4 (21) at a rate of 60 g/m². Prepare beds for planting during March and plant during April. Plant out plants 40 cm apart in the rows, with 50 cm between the rows. Mulch well with organic material like well-rotted compost. Water regularly and start foliar feeding with Kelpak or Nitrosol once plants start to flower, or start fertilising in September with general fertiliser like 3:1:5 (26) SR at a rate of 60 g/m scattered along the row.

## Q: What is the secret for growing avocados?

A: The avocado is an evergreen, tropical tree but can be grown in a sheltered position in more temperate regions. Avocados do not grow well in the winter rainfall areas. Trees will suffer from fruit drop if winter temperature and humidity are too low. They require deep, well-drained soil and regular watering in summer. Seedling trees are unreliable as they may take a very long time to start bearing. Grafted trees have to be planted to avoid disappointment. Feed during April, July and December with a general fertiliser like Wonder Flowers, Fruit and Shrubs at a rate of 60 g/m² scattered over the drip area. Keep the soil under trees mulched at all times and water regularly. Fruits do not ripen on the tree, but are ready to be picked when they are well developed. When stored at room temperature they will soften within eight to ten days. 'Fuerte' is an adaptable variety and will withstand temperatures of -2 °C without lasting damage. It bears pear-shaped fruit with a thin, dull-green, leathery skin. Other named varieties available are 'Hass', which bears egg-shaped fruit with a leathery, dark-purple skin; 'Pinkerton', which has dark-green, medium-sized, leathery-skinned fruit, and 'Simmons', which bears oval, smooth-skinned, light-green fruits.

## Q: What is a safe distance to plant a lemon tree from the house?

A: A distance of 5 m would be safe, with enough space for the tree to develop.

## Q: What is a tree tomato and where will it grow?

A: Tree tomato or Tamarillo is easily grown from seeds to form a small, umbrella-shaped tree up to 3 m tall. It needs a sunny, sheltered position and grows well in subtropical and frost-free, temperate regions. The fruit is egg-shaped with a tough skin and many seeds. Fruit must be skinned thinly and can be used to make chutney, to flavour stews and in salads. Fruit has a unique, acid-sweet flavour.

## Q: How are sweet potatoes grown?

A: Sweet potatoes require a light, well-drained soil and a warm growing season of four to six months. To plant sweet potatoes, they will need to be started by sprouted tubers, slips or rooted cuttings from September to December. Before planting, prepare the soil by applying a dressing of general fertiliser like Wonder Planting and Vegetables 2:3:4 (21) at a rate of 60 g/m². Plant 40 cm apart in rows that are 1 m apart and water regularly. Do not give additional fertiliser, as nitrogen will only promote leafy growth at the expense of the tubers. Wait until the plants are yellow before testing if tubers are mature. Tubers are ready to be harvested when the skin is firm and a cut surface dries white in a reasonably short time.

## Q: My rhubarb plants are no longer producing many leaves. I have had them in the same bed for at least seven years now. How can I rectify this problem?

A: Rhubarb is one of the few perennial vegetables and needs to be lifted and divided every three to four years to maintain productivity. The soil needs to be well drained. When preparing a new bed, add lots of organic material and a general fertiliser like Wonder Planting and Vegetables 2:3:4 (21) at a rate of 60 g/m². Divide plants in early spring, choosing only healthy and productive crowns for replanting. Mulch with well-rotted kraal manure every spring. Once plants are established, apply nitrogen fertiliser every four weeks throughout the active growing season. Stems are longer if grown in semi-shade. Do not allow plants to flower. If flower stems appear, cut them off at the base. When picking, always pull outer leaves with a downward and sideways action to break them away cleanly from the crown. Cut the leaves from the stems after picking and do not use any leaves, as rhubarb poisoning can occur.

## Q: I obtained two dozen one-year-old asparagus crowns which are growing very well. However, there are some plants that are producing very thin and spindly stems. Should I split the crowns of stronger growers to obtain more plants?

A: Asparagus is always raised from seeds and not by division of crowns. All unsatisfactory plants should be discarded. New plants can be raised from seeds sown in spring. Once established, asparagus crowns will keep on producing for many years. Production increases as plants grow older and reach full bearing after about five years. When planting crowns, set them about 20 cm deep in a trench, 50 cm apart in the row. Cover the crowns with 5 cm soil and fill in the trench as the plant grows. Water regularly and feed with nitrogen fertiliser during summer to promote lush foliage. Cut down yellow and dry stems at ground level in winter. Fertilise in late winter before spears appear, and do not cut any spears in the first

Spinach beet 'Bright Lights' is an excellent example of a vegetable that can be grown in the flower garden or used for added colour in a vegetable garden.

The globe artichoke (*Cynara scolymus*) is a very attractive herbaceous perennial with silver-grey foliage. The immature flower bud is edible.

year after planting. Start cutting spears only from three-year-old crowns. Green asparagus is cut from level beds and white spears are cut from beds that have had 30 cm soil put over the crowns (hills) during late winter. Cut these at about 15 cm below soil level when spear heads start to appear. Hills can be levelled in summer for cultivation and rebuilt in late winter for spring cutting.

**Q: I would like to grow six summer and six winter vegetables. Can you suggest some easier varieties to grow, as I am not an experienced gardener?**
A: For summer, grow beetroot, beans, cucumber, eggplant (brinjals), lettuce and tomatoes.

For winter, grow broccoli, cabbage, carrots, onions, peas and Swiss chard.

**Q: Which vegetables can be grown in flowerbeds in limited space?**
A: Radishes, beetroot, carrots and different types of lettuce can be planted in the front border. Asparagus and a few tomato plants can be grown scattered along the back of flowerbeds. Onions can be grown in small groups among flowers. Runner beans can be grown to cover a tepee-pole structure, made by tying three light poles together at the top, among taller flowering plants. Many herbs can be grown among and on the border of flowerbeds, for example parsley, chives, thyme, marjoram, basil and fennel.

**Q: Which vegetables need lots of water in dry weather?**
A: All vegetables suffer if a dry spell is prolonged, but those most susceptible to lack of water are peas, celery, spinach and lettuce.

**Q: Why do my tomatoes bear misshapen fruits? Is it a disease?**
A: Misshapen tomato fruits are not caused by a disease, but by sudden big differences in temper-

ature, usually during cold spells when the night-time temperature suddenly drops low and day temperatures are reasonably warm. If no more cold spells occur, the next batch of fruits will be normal.

**Q: What is a potager garden?**
A: It is a garden of formal design where vegetables and flowers are planted together.

**Q: Which herbs can be grown in a container on a patio?**
A: Most herbs can be grown in containers that are large enough. Bay trees make very attractive container plants and any annual herb can be grown around the rim of the container to act as a living mulch.

**Q: Which flowers are edible and can be used in salads?**
A: All flowers from culinary herbs. Edible garden and vegetable flowers are bean flowers, day lily (*Hemerocallis* spp.), English daisy (*Bellis perennis*), Japanese honeysuckle (*Lonicera japonica*), viola (*Viola tricolor*), lavender, marigold (*Tagetes tenuifolia*), nasturtium, pansy (*Viola wittrockiana*), pea flowers, feijoa, pinks (*Dianthus* spp.), radish flowers, roses (all but blue), rosemary, squash flowers, tulip (*Tulipa* spp.) and sweet violet (*Viola odorata*).

**Q: Which six perennial herbs would you suggest for the vegetable or flower garden?**
A: Chives, marjoram, mint, sage, tarragon and thyme.

**Q: What are the most common herbs for eating?**
A: Herbs used in cooking are: sweet basil for tomato sauces, pesto, soups and salads; chives for salads, sour cream and cottage cheese; dill for fish, shellfish and pickles; fennel for salads or as a cooked vegetable; marjoram for seasoning in stuffings, etc.; mints for teas and sauces; rosemary for seasoning roasts and chicken; sage for seasoning pork and dressings; summer savory for flavouring vegetables, particularly beans; thyme for seasoning in foods, salads and sauces; tarragon to flavour vinegar and chicken dishes.

**Q: Which herbs should I grow for making potpourri?**
A: The most common herbs for making potpourri are: angelica, bay laurel, bergamot (*Monarda didyma*), borage, calendula, catmint, chamomile, dianthus, eau de Cologne mint (*Mentha piperita* var. *citrata*), English lavender (*Lavandula angustifolia*), fennel, feverfew, French lavender (*Lavandula dentata*), lavender (*Lavandula vera*), lemon balm, lemon thyme, lemon verbena, marjoram, mints, oregano, rosemary, sage, scented geranium, Spanish lavender (*Lavandula stoechas*), summer savory, sweet basil, tansy, tarragon and thyme.

**Q: How can I cure herbs properly so as to retain flavour?**
A: Pick herb leaves and stems just before plants begin to flower, any time during the day after dew has disappeared. Dry them as quickly as possible in a warm, airy, well-ventilated place, without exposure to sunlight. Once leaves are completely dry and crisp, store in airtight containers.

**Q: Which herbs grow successfully indoors?**
A: The following herbs will grow indoors if plenty of light is available and the room is not too hot: basil, parsley, rosemary, marjoram, tarragon and lemon verbena.

# gardening
# for wildlife

The natural environment of wildlife is getting smaller and smaller because of land development, agricultural activities and pollution, with the result that gardens in urban and rural areas alike have become very valuable habitats for birds, lizards, insects like butterflies, and so on. Gardens with areas of woodland, shrubs and water have become sanctuaries, especially in times of drought. Wildlife in our gardens has a fragile existence and is dependent on the goodwill of the gardener. Any action the gardener takes to provide food and shelter will be reciprocated in natural biological control of garden pests like caterpillars, slugs, snails, mosquitoes and aphids, to name a few.

To get involved in conservation on a small scale we can all encourage wildlife into our gardens by planting indigenous plants, which are the natural source of food and shelter for birds, reptiles and insects. This does not mean that you have to destroy your existing garden and replant it with entirely indigenous plants. It involves the incorporation of certain indigenous plants to create a variety of bird and butterfly habitats within the garden. It is also vitally important not to use insecticides in the garden, because with no insect population your garden will also be bare of lizards, geckos, skinks and the colourful agama, not to mention many birds that all depend on insects to stay alive.

The best way to encourage wildlife into the garden is to incorporate a natural pond in a secluded area. Make it quite large, with shallow, sloping sides and flat, protruding stones for birds to perch on. Marginal water plants will also provide interest and cover for animals. If your garden is too small for a pond, include a birdbath instead. We should aim to let our gardens develop naturally, in tune with locally existing plants and natural factors like geology, soil and climate. In this way we will be able to contribute to a healthier habitat for everyone, including plants and animals for future generations.

## Planning your garden

An existing garden can easily be adapted to become more bird-friendly by incorporating indigenous plants that will provide natural food and shelter. When planning a new garden it will be easier, of course, to choose the right plants from the start. To attract as many bird species as possible you will have to provide a variety of habitats. These should include an open area, a natural water garden, a canopy area and a quiet, low-traffic area. The bigger the variety of food available, the greater the variety of birds attracted to the garden.

If you want birds to frequent your garden, it will be necessary to provide food for them using a safe feeding container with easy access.

## The open area

In most gardens the lawn is the largest open area, and is very valuable for birds like the hadeda, egret, plover, olive thrush, fiscal shrike and the Cape wagtail, all of which feed on the large variety of insects found in the lawn. They also need an open area where they can detect approaching danger quickly. It is important not to use insecticides on the lawn if caterpillars or crickets are noticed. Decide how severe the infestation is before resorting to insecticides. If it is a small infestation birds will be able to control the problem without any interference, but in cases of severe outbreaks of a pest, make sure to use the safest chemical so as not to poison insect-eating birds.

A good idea when planning the lawn area is to use ground covers to link a gravel and natural veld section with the shrub and tree areas. In this area you can provide a sand bath of about 1 m² in a well-drained patch filled with powdery sand. Birds like guinea fowl, mousebirds and sparrows, in particular, enjoy a good wallow in the sand. In the veld section you can provide indigenous grasses between rocks, for example *Eragrostis* spp. (lovegrass), *Panicum maximum* (buffalo grass), *Melinis nerviglumis* (bristle-leaved red top), *Melinis repens* (Natal red top) and *Miscanthus capensis* (dabagrass), which will provide weavers with grass to build their nests and colourful seed heads for birds to feed on.

The open area can include large sections of ground covers and low-growing shrubs, which will also be very attractive to butterflies and bees. Here are some examples: *Aptenia cordifolia* (heart leaf), *Arctotis* hybrids, *Bulbine frutescens* (stalked bulbine), *Carissa macrocarpa* 'Green Carpet' (dwarf Natal plum), *Carpobrotus deliciosus* (goukum), *Dymondia margaretae* (silver carpet), *Gazania* hybrids, *Geranium incanum* (carpet geranium), *Lampranthus* spp. (*Mesembryanthemum* spp. or vygies), *Osteospermum* hybrids, *Othonna* spp. (othonna), *Phyla nodiflora* (daisy lawn), *Phlox stolonifera* (creeping phlox), *Polygonum capitatum* (knotweed) and *Sedum acre* (wallpepper).

## The natural water garden

A pond with shallow, sloping sides and a variety of margin plants like bulrushes and water plants is the ideal way to attract wildlife to the garden. Provide enough cover for fish, frogs and other water creatures and flat, protruding stones for birds and insects like dragonflies to perch on. It is very easy to construct a natural water garden to resemble a miniature wetland with ready-made plastic sheeting. (See pages 107-117 for how to install a natural pond.)

The natural water garden should be located at the end of the open area, joining the low-traffic area so that it will have an open approach on one side and include dense vegetation on the other. The pond must have a shallow, sloping shelf on one side for smaller birds to bathe in. The secret is to imitate nature as closely as possible, incorporating logs, natural rocks, a thick, sandy bottom and water plants to cover at least half the water surface. Rocks will provide the ideal place for reptiles like lizards to sun themselves. The pond should also include indigenous fish like the banded tilapia to keep the mosquito and frog populations in check, as they feed on larvae and tadpoles. Unlike ordinary goldfish, these fish are not easy prey for birds like the kingfisher or hamerkop. Weavers will enjoy nesting in papyrus and bulrushes close to the water.

If a pond is beyond your means any shallow container will be ideal to serve as a birdbath. Make sure to place these in more protected areas at ground level for shy birds. A birdbath on a pedestal should also not be placed in the open, as many birds are too shy to visit an exposed birdbath. Doves and pigeons like to drink regularly and, together with sparrows, are the most common bird species to utilise exposed birdbaths.

## The canopy area

This is the area provided by trees and large shrubs. It is a very important area for nesting, roosting and feeding. Be sure to provide evergreen, well-foliaged trees as well as deciduous trees and try to incorporate as many fruit-, berry-, seed- and nectar-producing plants as possible to provide food for birds and butterflies.

Most birds and butterflies prefer indigenous plants for nesting and feeding activities. It is important to plant trees and shrubs that will provide food and nectar throughout the year, and not only in spring or summer. This can be difficult in smaller gardens, and a good idea is to provide additional food for birds by means of bird feeders. Plant a variety of nectar-producing plants to attract sunbirds, bulbuls, Cape white-eye and the Cape sugarbird to the garden.

Some excellent indigenous fruit-, berry- and seed-bearing trees to consider are: *Berchemia zeyheri* (red ivory), *Bridelia micrantha* (mitzeerie), *Celtis africana* (white stinkwood), *Dovyalis zeyheri* (wild apricot), *Ekebergia capensis* (Cape ash), *Ficus* spp.

The following are for large gardens only: *Halleria lucida* (tree fuchsia), *Harpephyllum caffrum* (wild plum), *Ilex mitis* (wild holly), *Kiggelaria africana* (wild peach), *Ochna natalitia* (Natal plane), *Olea europaea* subsp. *africana* (wild olive), *Pappea capensis* (jacket plum), *Phoenix reclinata* (wild date palm), *Rhus* spp. (karree varieties), *Strelitzia nicolai* (Natal wild banana), *Syzygium guineense* (water pear).

Nectar-producing indigenous trees are: *Aloe bainesii* (tree aloe), *Erythrina* spp. (coral tree varieties), *Gardenia* varieties, *Halleria lucida* (tree fuchsia), *Kigelia africana* (sausage tree), *Schotia brachypetala* (weeping boer bean), *Turraea floribunda* (wild honeysuckle tree).

Wild irises (*Dietes bicolor*) growing as a ground cover beneath a canopy of large trees.

*Leonotis leonurus* is a hardy, indigenous nectar-producing plant.

Indigenous fruit-bearing shrubs to consider are: *Carissa macrocarpa* (Natal plum), *Dovyalis caffra* (Kei apple), *Ehretia rigida* (puzzle bush), *Grewia occidentalis* (cross-berry), *Maytenus* spp., *Myrsine africana* (Cape myrtle), *Ochna serrulata* (plane bush), *Rhamnus prinoides* (dogwood), *Rhus* spp.

Indigenous nectar-producing shrubs, perennials and bulbs are: *Agapanthus* spp., *Alberta magna* (Natal flame bush), *Aloe* spp., *Bauhinia galpinii* (pride of De Kaap), *Clivia* spp., *Crotolaria capensis* (Cape rattlepod), *Erica* spp., *Gardenia* spp., *Greyia sutherlandii* (Natal bottlebrush), *Halleria elliptica* (wild fuchsia), *Kniphofia* spp. (red-hot poker), *Leonotis leonurus* (lion's ear), *Melianthus major* (honey bush), *Leucospermum* spp. (pincushion proteas), *Phygelius capensis* (Cape fuchsia), *Plumbago auriculata* (blue plumbago), *Protea* spp., *Salvia africana-lutea* (beach salvia), *Strelitzia reginae* (crane flower), *Tecomaria capensis* (Cape honeysuckle), *Wachendorfia thrysiflora* (bloodroot), *Watsonia* spp.

## A secluded, low-traffic area

This area is usually located in the most remote part of the garden and should be kept wild and natural, without any interference from gardeners. Plant indigenous acacia thorn trees on the perimeter, with dense shrubs underneath and in front of these trees to form a 6-m-thick bushy area. Provide thick mulch of organic material and loose rocks or stones to support a thriving insect population. Birds like robins, shrikes, bokmakieries, thrushes and coucals will appreciate this undisturbed area in which to forage for tasty morsels at ground level. Cover the fence with creepers like *Senecio tamoides* (canary creeper) or *Rhoicissus tomentosa* (forest grape). Consider planting a hedge rather than putting up a concrete wall. Plant a hedge of *Dovyalis caffra* (Kei apple), *Carissa macrocarpa* (Natal plum) or *Rhamnus prinoides* (dogwood) on your boundary to provide thick cover for shy birds.

## Bird feeders

If you want birds to frequent your garden regularly, it will usually be necessary to feed them during the lean winter months when fruits, berries, insects and nectar-producing flowers are scarce. The best way of feeding birds is to provide safe feeding areas, like a special table or hanging container, with easy access. By providing food randomly you will prevent birds from becoming entirely dependent on you. You can reduce the amount of food provided during spring and summer as soon as you notice that it stays untouched.

To encourage a variety of birds you will have to provide food at different areas throughout the garden, as bolder birds like starlings, sparrows and doves will dominate the feeding table if there is only one feeding area.

*Constructing a feeding table*
It is easy to construct a feeding table. Either mount a wooden board (with a collar to prevent rats and mice from stealing the food) on a pole, or suspend it from a branch so that cats cannot reach it. Nail a skirting all round to prevent food from falling off and provide nails to hold fruits. A roof is useful to protect food from the sun and rain but is not essential.

The feeding table can also be secured to the kitchen windowsill. It is not necessary to have very elaborate bird feeders; any method of providing food for birds will be accepted.

A variety of foods will attract birds. Large pieces (rather than crumbs) of stale brown bread and fruitcake soaked in water are very popular. Pieces of fruit, especially apples, pears, pawpaws, grapes, guavas and oranges, can be pushed onto nails to encourage barbets, bulbuls, starlings, white-eyes and mousebirds. Any seeds, nuts and grains will be popular with seed-eaters. Insect eaters can be fed large bones with pieces of meat still attached to them, and mealworms, chopped-up bacon and cheese rinds, suet, butcher's bone meal and dog food are excellent. You can also make up special 'bird pudding' by making moulds of melted suet mixed with seeds, nuts, pieces of dried fruit and crumbs and placing them in the freezer to set. Put out small quantities of the pudding on a weekly basis.

## Providing nesting sites

Most large gardens, especially those with indigenous plants, will have enough natural nesting sites and nesting material available. Many hole-nesting birds, however, can be encouraged to nest in provided nesting logs and nest boxes in young or small gardens where there are not enough large trees and dense bushes available. Birds like barbets, woodpeckers, starlings, hoopoes and owls will be likely species to make use of provided nesting sites placed at strategic positions in the garden. Always secure a nesting box or log firmly in place, at least 2 m or higher above the ground with the entrance facing away from the sun and prevailing wind direction. Nesting logs may be solid or hollowed out beforehand. Barbets and woodpeckers will prefer solid logs, as they like to excavate their own nests. Remember to check the condition of nesting boxes and logs between seasons and do repairs, as leaking boxes or logs will not be used again. Never look into a nesting log or box during the breeding season, as breeding birds can easily be scared away and leave the nest permanently.

A lesser doublecollared sunbird feeding on the nectar of *Agapanthus inapertus*.

Nest boxes vary in design according to the needs of different bird species. Some birds, for example the spotted eagle owl, prefer a more open box, while others, like the hoopoe, prefer a closed box with a very small opening. Long wooden blocks nailed to the wall behind a creeper are also very popular nesting sites for birds like the robin, wagtail, sparrow or dove. You can also provide a wooden shelf under the overhang of the roof for swallows and rock martins.

## Gardening for butterflies

Butterflies are not only beautiful but also very important in any garden, as they are pollinators of many flowers and attract birds who prey on them. To encourage butterflies into the garden you will have to plant nectar-producing plants and larval host plants. Remember not to use insecticides to rid your garden of caterpillars, as these will be dealt with by birds. The rest will become butterflies or moths, which are also preyed on by birds and reptiles. Many of the larger nectar-producing flowers are preferred by nectar-feeding birds, while the smaller fragrant and tubular flowers attract butterflies. Most butterflies are seasonal because they are dependent on the flowering period of their preferred food-providing plants, which usually are indigenous. In addition to providing indigenous host plants you can also attract butterflies by sowing special butterfly mix, made up of seeds of annual plants preferred by butterflies.

Nectar-producing indigenous plants which are a must for butterflies are: *Asystasia gangetica* (creeping foxglove), *Barleria* spp. (bush violets), *Buddleja davidii* (butterfly bush), *Heteropyxis natalensis* (lavender tree), *Hypoestes aristata* (ribbon bush), *Orthosiphon labiatus* (pink sage).

Indigenous larval host plants to plant in the garden are the following:

Ground covers and perennials: *Asclepias fruticosa* (milkweed), *Asystasia gangetica* (creeping foxglove), low-growing *Plectranthus* spp., *Setaria megaphylla* (broad-leaved bristle grass), *Stapelia rufa* (carrion flower).

Shrubs and climbers: *Burchellia bubalina* (wild pomegranate), *Chrysanthemoides monilifera* (brother berry or bush-tick berry), *Crotalaria capensis* (Cape rattlepod), *Grewia occidentalis* (cross-berry), *Indigofera* spp., *Jasminum angulare* (wild jasmine), *Mackaya bella* (forest bell bush), *Plumbago auriculata* (blue plumbago), *Thunbergia alata* (black-eyed Susan).

Trees: *Acacia karroo* (sweet thorn), *Calodendrum capense* (Cape chestnut), *Clerodendrum glabrum* (stinkleaf tree), *Dracaena alteriformis* (dragon tree), *Ficus* spp. (wild figs), *Hibiscus tiliaceus* (wild cotton tree), *Kiggelaria africana* (wild peach), *Vepris undulata* (white ironwood), *Xylotheca kraussiana* (African dog rose), *Ziziphus mucronata* (buffalo thorn).

## Questions and answers

**Q: How can we ensure that cats don't prey on birds in the garden?**
A: Feed your cat in the morning to ensure that it will not go out hunting during the day. Cat collars with bells are available to warn birds of approaching danger. If neighbouring cats are a problem you will have to enclose your property with a wire-mesh fence. Grow indigenous creepers against the fence to attract birds and butterflies. Make sure that feeding tables are out of reach of hungry cats.

**Q: When is it necessary to clean a natural pond in the garden, and how is this done?**

Besides being beautiful, butterflies are also pollinators of many flowers and attract birds which prey on them.

A: A natural pond with healthy plants and fish should not be cleaned at all, because the delicate balance in the water ecosystem will be destroyed. If the pond is very shallow – less than 40 cm deep – it will probably need cleaning, as the water temperature fluctuates too much and it will not be able to sustain a healthy water ecosystem. Flush the pond with rainwater and remove silt when necessary, but try not to disturb the natural pond unnecessarily.

**Q: Which are the most common insect-eating birds to attract to the garden for biological control?**
A: In the open area of the garden, swifts and swallows that feed on flying insects. Hadedas on the lawn feed on worms, Parktown prawns, crickets, snails and slugs. Plovers, hoopoes and the sacred ibis will also feed on worms on the lawn. The fiscal shrike, the paradise flycatcher and the fork-tailed drongo feed on most flying insects. The Cape white-eye and the crombec will feed on aphids. The spotted eagle owl feeds on insects attracted to a light during the night. Robins, bokmakieries, thrushes and coucals will feed on caterpillars, snails, slugs, etc. under thick shrubs and in the mulch layer between plants.

**Q: Which exotic nectar-producing or berry-bearing shrubs can be planted to attract birds to the garden?**
A: Suitable exotic shrubs are: *Abutilon* hybrids (Chinese lantern), *Arbutus unedo* (strawberry tree), *Callistemon* spp. (bottlebrush varieties), *Cotoneaster* spp., *Crataegus* spp. (hawthorn), *Feijoa sellowiana* (pineapple guava), *Grevillea* hybrids, *Ilex* spp. (holly), *Russelia equisetiformis* (coralbush), *Salvia rutilans* (pineapple sage), *Sambucus* spp. (elderberry), *Syzygium paniculatum* (brush cherry).

**Q: I have put up a bird feeder close to my kitchen window, but birds do not like to feed there. How can I encourage them to feed at the feeding table?**
A: You will have to make the birds used to you by feeding them in a secluded, quiet spot, then gradually moving the feeding table closer to the house. Once they are accustomed to taking food from it you can safely place it at your kitchen window.

**Q: The wild peach tree in my garden gets covered in caterpillars every summer. Why does this only happen to this tree and not to other plants as well?**
A: The wild peach tree (*Kiggelaria africana*) is the host plant to the *Acraea horta* butterfly, which lays its eggs on the leaves. The caterpillars hatch in vast numbers and can defoliate young trees quite fast. It does no harm to the plant but serves to stimulate new growth after an attack. It is one of nature's ways of pruning trees. These caterpillars will attract cuckoos to the garden, as they like to feed on them. No insecticide should be used, as these caterpillars are present for only a short time.

**Q: I am trying not to use any pesticides in my garden, but every year the amaryllis borer caterpillars nearly destroy my clivia and amaryllis plants. How should I go about dealing with this problem?**
A: There are certain bird species that feed on these caterpillars. It will also help a lot if you can plant a large clump of the natural host plant for the moth that causes the problem. Plant indigenous albuca bulbs to entice the moth away from your clivia and amaryllis plants. You can also spray your plants with wormwood/garlic spray once a week from September to April. The only environment-friendly way to rid your clivias of these caterpillars is to remove them by hand.

This informal pond is perfectly suited to the natural surroundings.

# water gardening

Water is hypnotic and fascinating and has always been a basic feature of gardens from the earliest gardening times. A natural pond, for example, creates a feeling of tranquillity and restfulness. Water is a garden feature that reflects everything around it, thereby acquiring a third dimension. The relaxing sound of moving water and the life that it attracts and sustains makes the water garden as desirable as a patio or a lawn. A well-designed reflecting pond is an asset to any garden. It can transform an ordinary garden into an extraordinary showpiece.

Water gardening and water features have become a very popular trend in recent years, thanks to the availability of flexible plastic liners, inexpensive pumps, prefabricated ponds, cascades, water plants and fish. These products have placed water features within reach of all and sundry. Whether you have a small flat with a balcony, a townhouse or a large garden, there will be a size, shape and style to suit you.

## Planning your water feature

It is very important to plan carefully before starting out to build or install your water feature. Remember that any water feature needs care and maintenance. Choose a feature that you will be able to cope with. The larger and more ornate it is, the more maintenance there will be. Consider the following basic points to help you decide on a water feature:

**Style.** Here you will have to decide on the size of the water feature you want and what the purpose of the feature should be. The size of your pond will be dictated by your garden dimensions: it should complement your garden and not dominate it. Do you want a formal feature, a natural, informal water feature like a bog garden, or a small feature like a millstone? Available space and the style of the house and garden will be the determining factors here.

**Position.** The best position for a water feature will be determined by its style and function. You will obviously choose a spot clearly visible from where you spend most of your time, and if you want to hear the sound of water, the water feature will have to be close to your living area. If, for example, you want to attract wildlife to your garden an informal pond or bog garden in a secluded, low-lying and sunny area would be ideal.

**Microclimate.** The microclimate of the chosen area is important. Is it in full sun or in the shade? Is it very hot or cold? Remember the function of your water feature when deciding its position. If you want water lilies, the pond will need at least six hours of full sun, and if you want Koi fish you will need some shade as well as full sun.

**Features.** Decide which features will best enhance your pond, for example a statue, waterfall, fountain or water plants. The site and function of your pond will help to determine the choice. If your site is on a natural slope, a waterfall will obviously work well for you.

A fun water feature installed in half barrels and highly suitable for small gardens.

**The cost.** The amount of money you want to spend will determine the water feature you install. A more complex feature with a waterfall and fountain will obviously cost much more than a more simple feature like a plastic-lined natural pond.

## The formal pond

A formal water feature can be either modern or classic, depending on the architecture of the home and the space available. Formal ponds are usually constructed with durable material like bricks, cement and tiles. There are, however, formal and classic pond moulds available these days. Remember these guidelines when designing a formal pond:

- Keep the design simple and uncluttered.
- A formal pond always follows geometric lines and is symmetrical.
- It may have a focal point, such as an ornamental statue or fountain which may be multitiered, placed symmetrically for a classic style or asymmetrically for a modern pond.
- A formal pond always has a well-defined border or edging.
- The classic pond is usually enhanced by one or more of the following: symmetrical plantings, columns, arches, containers and trelliswork.

## The informal pond

An informal pond has a free form with gentle curves and no straight lines, and the size can be anything from very small to very large. Flexible black plastic sheeting and prefabricated plastic or fibre-cement moulds have become very popular for this type of pond, as opposed to the more expensive cement-constructed ponds. Informal ponds include the natural pond, the reflecting pond and the bog garden, as well as prefabricated ponds with or without waterfalls, and water features like millstones, rock pools, etc. An informal natural pond, waterfall or bog garden has to look as if it has been lifted out of nature into your garden. Here, the water and surrounding plants and rocks must merge together without visible borders.

## Pond installation

How to install a natural pond using pond liner or plastic sheeting:

1.  Use a hosepipe or rope to outline the shape of your pond. Remember that simple designs always look better when finished. A shape with too many curves and corners is not suitable as it wastes too much lining material and does not look pleasing. To calculate the size of the liner, measure the maximum width and maximum length and add twice the maximum pool depth to both the length and the width of the pond. (Example: If your pond is 2 m wide, 3 m long and 50 cm deep, you will need a liner of about 3 m x 4 m.) Remember to add the overlap for the rim edging to both the length and width. Choose a pond size that will correspond with a standard pond liner width.
2.  Mark the outline with sand and start to dig the hole. Start digging in the middle of the pond to the required depth (a depth of 50 cm is sufficient for fish and water lilies). Create a planting shelf (20 cm deep and wide

This formal pond follows symmetrical lines and has a gravel surround. Note the glazed pot used as a focal point and the colourful container plants.

from the rim) around the edge if you want to put in marginal water plants like arum lilies or bulrushes. Remember to shape the sides with a slight slope to prevent soil from falling in.

3. Make sure that the rim of the pond is level on all sides. Use a straight plank that is long enough to reach the rim all round, put your spirit level on the plank and adjust the rim until it is level. Prepare the rim for the edging you want. Remove protruding stones or roots and fill the hole with soil.

4. Line the surface of the hole all over with a 5-cm layer of damp sand. It is a good idea to line the bottom with undercarpet felt or old carpet.

5. Spread the liner carefully over the hole and position it so that it is centred. Allow the plastic liner to touch the bottom of the pond. Do not stand on the liner. A good idea is to do this on a hot, sunny day, as the liner material will become more flexible and easier to work with. Make sure that you retain at least 20 cm all round for the rim edging. Hold the liner in position with smooth stones around the top.

6. Start filling the pond with water. Smooth the liner and make the pleats tidy all round as the water level rises. Close off the water when it is about 10 cm below the rim.

7. Finish the edging around the rim by laying slabs or smooth stones on the prepared rim, or bury the overlapping edge of the liner to a depth of at least 10 cm in a shallow trench. Be sure to cover the plastic completely to protect it from the sun's ultra-violet rays.

8. Complete your pond by placing your pump and fountain or waterfall, and finish off with water and bog plants. Moving water and water plants will help to keep the pond clean. Make sure that water plants never shade more than two-thirds of your pond. Initially, the pond water may be murky, but this will change with time as the water plants get established.

9. Fill the pond with water to the top.

10. Fish can be introduced once plants have settled in.

# Water plants

To maintain a healthy pond which is clean and clear, the correct balance between water plants and algae is essential. Water plants compete with algae for nutrients, especially nitrates from rotting plant material and fish droppings. Water plants also exchange carbon dioxide in water for oxygen, which is essential for fish. By shading at least half the pond they prevent sunlight from encouraging algae growth.

Water plants include oxygenating, deep-water, floating, marginal and marsh plants. Fish should only be introduced once oxygenating plants are established and flourishing. The reason is that fish like to nibble on oxygenating plants and if these plants are not given enough time to become established, the fish will destroy them as well as the balance in the pond.

The planting up of your pond should be done in summer when the water is warm enough for water plants to grow and flower. The best way of having plants in your pond is to plant them into special plastic mesh containers.

## Oxygenating plants

Oxygenating plants are important as they provide food, shelter, oxygen and a spawning medium for fish. These plants, also known as pondweed, are anchored with coarse gravel in mesh containers and will quickly establish roots if left undisturbed. Nine to ten bunches of oxygenating plants for every square metre of pond surface will be sufficient to maintain a healthy pond. Listed below are a few oxygenating plants:

*Ceratophyllum demersum* (hornwort) grows in dense plumes of dark-green leaves and thrives in deep, cold and shaded ponds.

*Elodea crispa* is a very good producer of oxygen and forms sturdy stems covered with curled leaves.

*Potamogeton* spp. (pondweed) has branching stems with long leaves and is larger-growing than other oxygenating plants.

*Ranunculus aquatilis* (water crowfood) has very fine foliage underwater and lobed leaves on the water surface. It bears small, white flowers in spring.

*Myriophyllum* spp. (milfoil and parrot's feather) should be avoided as they are very invasive. Parrot's feather has already been declared a noxious weed.

## Floating plants

These are not as effective as oxygenating plants and, unlike them, do not need anchorage. They are free-floating on the surface and discourage algae by cutting out sunlight, which is essential for algae growth. They are usually grown for their ornamental value and can proliferate very quickly. Many floating plants, however, are declared weeds and should be avoided, for example: *Eichhornia crassipes* (water hyacinth), *Pistia stratiotes* (water lettuce) and *Salvinia molesta* (Kariba weed). *Azolla* spp. (water fern or floating fairy moss) has lovely purple and red tints during autumn, but can also be very invasive and should never be allowed to enter free-flowing streams, rivers or dams.

Indigenous arum lilies are outstanding marginal plants. This hybrid, *Zantedeschia* 'Green Goddess', has variegated blooms.

## Deep-water plants

These plants usually have floating foliage on the water surface and are essential for maintaining the correct balance in the pond. They shade the water and prevent the sun from reaching algae, they provide shelter for fish and other small water animals and they are usually very ornamental. Deep-water plants like water lilies need to be planted up in a heavy soil without any organic material, as this would only encourage algae to flourish. Use special plastic mesh containers for this purpose. Cover the soil surface with coarse gravel or small stones to prevent fish from removing the soil. One plant for every 2,5 m² of pond surface is sufficient to maintain a healthy balance. Some excellent deep-water plants are:

*Nymphaea* spp. (water lilies), the most beautiful of all water plants. Flower colours range from white, yellow, blue and pink to red. Water lily varieties differ in that some grow very vigorously, while others need shallower water and a smaller area. It is important to choose the correct variety for your pond size and depth. Different varieties will grow best in water depths from 30 cm to 80 cm.

*\*Aponogeton distachyos* (Cape pondweed or 'waterblommetjie') has dark-green, strap-like leaves and bears scented, white flowers with black anthers from July to December. It will grow in water from 20 cm to 60 cm deep.

*Orontium aquaticum* (golden club) is versatile in that it will grow in shallow pond margins and in 60-cm-deep ponds. In deep water foliage tends to float, while in pond margins the leaves grow upright. Leaves are an attractive, velvety dark green on the upper side with a silvery reverse. White-stemmed flower spikes with many tiny yellow flowers appear during spring and early summer.

## Marginal and marsh plants

These are plants that grow in marginal areas of ponds, in water up to a depth of 20 cm. There are many different varieties, from small to very large, available for this purpose. It is very important to choose the right plants for your particular pond size. One-third of the pond margin should be covered with marginal plants to give a balanced effect. Some popular marginal plants are:

*Acorus gramineus* 'Variegata', a grass-like perennial with striped cream-and-green foliage, excellent in sun or shade.

*Cyperus* spp. (papyrus and sedge grass), perennial clump-forming plants that are equally happy in and out of the water.

*Gunnera manicata*, a deciduous perennial with enormous leaves and brown flowers.

*Iris* spp. (Louisiana iris, Japanese iris, yellow flag iris). These water irises are lovely when in flower.

*Lobelia cardinalis* (cardinal flower) has bronze-coloured foliage and red flowers, and is a lovely plant for colour contrast.

*Myosotis scorpioides* (water forget-me-not), a spreading perennial with lovely, light-blue flowers during summer.

*Pontederia cordata* (arrow-leaf or pickerel weed), a lovely plant with glossy, light-green, upright foliage and blue flowers in autumn.

*Scirpus cernuus* (cat's whiskers), a densely tufted rush-like plant, ideal for smaller water features.

*\*Zantedeschia aethiopica* (white arum lily). These lovely indigenous plants are outstanding marginal plants with their lush, green foliage and white flower spathes.

An informal pond with a free form and a large size, suitable only for a very large garden.

# Questions and answers

**Q: I would like to build an informal pond close to my patio. What is the minimum size for a pond if I want to keep fish and water plants?**

A: For fish, plants and clear water the absolute minimum size to consider would be 1,8 m x 1,2 m x 0,4 m.

**Q: Which trees can I grow close to water and in places that are sometimes very wet?**

A: *Taxodium distichum* (swamp cypress) and, for frost-free areas, the indigenous *Barringtonia racemosa* (powder-puff tree), *Acer palmatum* (Japanese maple) and *Hibiscus tiliaceus* (lagoon hibiscus) would be very good choices.

**Q: I would like an unusual, smallish water feature for my patio, but I do not want a ready-made, mould-type feature. Could you give me a few ideas about what to use and how to go about assembling it?**

A: You could utilise any type of container like a wooden barrel, ceramic pot, ethnic pot, clay urn, unusual bowl, pipes or a metal watering can. When choosing your container, make sure that it is leakproof and made of durable material. Wood, for example, will have to be treated. Use a good pump, slightly larger than you think will be necessary. Let water cascade out of one container into another. For example, to assemble a feature with an upside-down, glazed ceramic pot that has to work on the same principle as a millstone, you will need at least two containers – where one can be underground with the pump to circulate the water – enough pebbles and stones for the water to drain through and a glazed pot placed upside down, where the water can bubble out of the central hole and cascade down the sides. With a little imagination you can experiment with many different ideas to come up with a really unusual water feature.

A lovely informal pond with an Oriental theme, placed close to the patio.

**Q: How can I enhance an old water feature that is informal in style and full of pondweed and water lilies?**

A: Firstly, clear out everything from your pond and clean it thoroughly. If you want to retain some water lilies, do this in summer. You can replant water lilies in special plastic mesh baskets. Oxygenating plants can also be replanted into mesh baskets. Once plants are established, goldfish can be introduced. Install a pump for a fountain. You could choose different fountainheads to provide, for example, a bubbling jet, a bell jet or a spray jet. Most fountainheads can be changed; you will just have to make sure that the pump is the right size for handling the fountainhead. To enhance your fountain even more you can also install a fountain light to light it up at night. Remember that water lilies do not tolerate water on the surface of their leaves for long periods, so make sure that the fountain does not splash onto your water lily leaves.

**Q: I would like to grow Louisiana irises in my pond. Could you give me some information on how to grow them?**

A: Louisiana irises are native to the Mississippi delta and many hybrids are available in colours ranging from black, purple, blue, red, orange, salmon, pink and yellow to white. Some varieties are ruffled, some are smooth and some have pronounced veining on the flowers. Plant these irises in late summer and autumn in special plastic mesh baskets with slow-release phosphate fertiliser. Make sure that the rhizome is at least 15 cm underwater. They will multiply quickly and will need to be divided every three years. Plants need a few hours of full sun to flower and in hot regions should be shaded in the afternoon. They also make ideal cut flowers during spring.

A natural water feature of good proportion with well-established water and marginal plants.

**Q: Could you please list some indigenous water plants to grow in the pond and around the margin?**

A: **Deep-water plants and floating plants:** *Nymphaea nouchali* var. *caerulea* (water lily) bears blue flowers in mid- to late summer; *Nymphoides indica*, the small, yellow water lily, flowers during summer; *Aponogeton angustifolius* bears white flowers in winter; *Aponogeton distachyos* (Cape pondweed or 'waterblommetjie') bears scented, white flowers from July to December; *Lobelia capillifolia* is a perennial with light-blue flowers in spring and summer.

**Margin and marsh plants:** Restios (reed-like plants found in fynbos) such as *Chondropetalum mucronatum*, which grows 2 m tall and forms a thick-stemmed tussock; *Elegia capensis* (broom reed), clump-forming and up to 2 m tall; *Elegia equisetacea*, a spreading plant which grows up to 1 m tall. Restios resemble grasses as they also form tussocks, but differ from grasses in that male and female flowers are on separate plants. They make excellent feature plants. *Crinum bulbispermum* (Orange River lily) is a deciduous bulb with grey-green foliage and large, pink, trumpet-shaped flowers in spring; *Crinum campanulatum* (water crinum), green, strap-like foliage and deep-pink, lily-like flowers in spring; *Cyathea dregei* (common tree fern), a large fern for full sun or semi-shade moist conditions; *Cyperus* spp. – many papyrus varieties are available; *Gomphostigma virgatum* (otter bush), an evergreen shrub with masses of small, white flowers in summer, needs full sun; *Kniphofia uvaria* (red-hot poker), an evergreen perennial with reddish buds that open to orange-yellow to greenish-yellow flowers in full sun; *Lobelia anceps*, a perennial with lush, green foliage and light-blue flowers, sun to shade; *Mentha longifolia* (wild mint), a rhizomatous perennial with white to mauve flowers in summer; *Phygelius aequalis*, a fast-growing perennial with tall spikes of drooping, yellow, tubular flowers in summer, sun to semi-shade; *Phygelius capensis* (Cape fuchsia), a fast-growing perennial with spikes of tubular, red flowers; *Schizostylis coccinea* (crimson flag or scarlet river lily), a bulb with strap-like foliage and star-shaped, scarlet-pink flowers in summer; *Wachendorfia thrysiflora* (bloodroot), an evergreen, bulbous plant with pleated foliage and tall spikes with yellow flowers in summer; *Zantedeschia aethiopica* (white arum lily), a fast-growing perennial with lush, green foliage and lovely, white, spathe-like flowers in winter, spring and early summer.

**Q: Could you give me some advice about the sacred lotus?**

A: The sacred lotus (*Nelumbo nucifera*) is a vigorous water plant that thrives in subtropical areas. It grows in shallow margins and boggy areas. The leaves are circular and grow well above the water. It bears large, creamy-white flowers with pink tips in summer. The fruit resembles the rose of a watering can and is very popular with flower arrangers. It dies down in winter and is easily propagated from seeds or division of tubers. Plant tubers in a large plastic or terracotta pot and fill with good garden loam, enriched with kraal manure. Cover the soil surface with coarse river sand and submerge the pot in no less than 30 cm of water. Give them enough space as they spread very quickly. Lotus can also be grown in a large pot without drainage holes and placed near the patio. Always keep the pot well watered.

**Q: I have been told that maintaining a water feature involves a lot of effort, as pond plants always spread very quickly. Is this true?**

A: Most water plants spread quickly. It should not be a problem, as most are oxygenating plants that provide oxygen for wildlife and fish and also reduce the formation of algae. You can easily remove some of these plants as soon as the pond looks congested, using a spring-tined rake. Always leave enough behind to cover at least two-thirds of the water space with water plants.

This well-positioned millstone ideally complements the style and size of the garden and house.
Note the soft *Helichrysum petiolatum* spilling over the steps.

# pots and containers

Pots and containers are a very convenient way of planting for patios, poolsides, balconies, verandas, courtyards and small areas, for instance in urban townhouse gardens. Container gardening is the art of growing plants in an artificial environment and is suitable for virtually any plant and position. In recent years it has become a very exciting form of gardening because of the huge variety of shapes and sizes, textures, materials and plants available. Container gardening is sometimes the only way of growing plants with specific soil requirements or in arid regions. It is also much easier to water container plants and to move the pot or container to another area, depending on the seasonal climate.

Pots and containers are widely used to add distinction to a certain spot, for example on either side of an entrance or at the top and bottom of steps, or against a dark-green background. A sculptured or glazed pot can also be used to great effect as a focal point in the garden. Containers can be used just about anywhere in a garden and will fit any garden style because there are so many different designs available.

## Choosing a container

Follow these basic principles when choosing containers to achieve a successful display:

- The container must suit the growth habit of the plant; in other words, the pot or container must be large enough for the chosen plant. For example, do not try to grow plants larger than annuals, bulbs or perennials in a bowl, or a floribunda rose bush in a pot smaller than 45 cm in diameter.
- The plant must be in proportion to the size of the container, which must be one-third of the overall height and diameter of the plant and container together.
- Choose a natural colour that blends in with the surroundings. The function of the container is to set the plant off to maximum effect; it should not compete with the plant. Consider the natural, unglazed look of terracotta pots or choose a good-quality exterior PVA paint in earthy colours for fibre-cement pots.
- Do not try to fit as many containers as possible into a certain area; rather space them well apart so that each plant can make a statement on its own. Group them according to shape and colour; try not to mix too many different shapes, materials and colours.
- To help you choose the right size for a sculptured container – like a classic urn, for example – that has to

Pots and containers are perfect for patios and this example shows the balance which can be obtained by correct grouping and in combination with patio furniture.

Using a strawberry pot is an excellent way of producing fruit in a confined space.

serve as a focal point, pile up some bricks in the spot where the urn is needed and scale it up or down until the correct proportion for the site is reached.

■ Make sure that whatever container you use for planting up, has a decent-sized hole in the bottom for drainage.

■ Use the correct size of drip tray or pot feet indoors or on special patio tiles outdoors. Pots look much better without drip trays, as too large a drip tray is unsightly. They also retain water during and after rain, causing pots to become waterlogged.

■ Group containers according to the plants' mature size, with taller plants towards the back or middle and the shortest plants in front or towards the sides.

A wide variety of containers is available, from straightforward plastic, clay and fibre-cement pots to ornamental and sculptured containers, glazed pots and bowls. Terracotta clay pots are porous, which is to the advantage of plants but also means that the potting mix dries out faster. In time it will acquire a natural look, with moss and lichen growing on the outside. White salts may also appear on the surface and can be scrubbed off if you don't like it. When using some rural ethnic clay pots, remember to line the inside with plastic sheeting to protect the pot from constant moisture. As these pots were not fired at very high temperatures they may crack or break easily when exposed to all weather conditions.

Glazed pots exposed to outside weather conditions will be liable to crazing (forming of fine cracks). To protect the glaze you should paint the glazed surface with a tile sealer or silicone wax. You can also use a plastic pot inside your glazed pot to prevent salts from the potting mix seeping under the glaze and damaging it. The potting mix will not dry out as quickly as in porous pots.

Wooden containers and baskets need to be treated against decay and ants before planting into them; it is a good idea to use a plastic sheet to line the inside of these containers. Make sure that the plastic has sufficient holes for drainage at the bottom.

Bear in mind that anything that will hold enough potting mix and has a drainage hole is a suitable container for a plant to grow in. Many gardeners find inspiration in an old, unused wheelbarrow, a sink, bath, trough, fire-grate, tin or hollowed-out tree stump, which is fine, as long as these containers blend in with the surrounding garden.

## The potting mix

The health and vigour of a plant depends largely on the quality of the potting mix. It must be of the right texture for optimum root development, contain all the essential nutrients for plant growth, retain moisture and drain well. Modern potting soils fulfil all these requirements and are readily available from most reputable garden centres and nurseries countrywide.

You can also make up your own potting mixture by mixing together the following:

- seven parts (by volume) of good garden loam for nutrients;
- three parts (by volume) of sieved, well-decomposed compost or peat moss for moisture retention and nutrients;
- two parts (by volume) of well-rotted kraal manure for nutrients;
- two parts (by volume) of river sand for drainage.

To every three buckets (10-litre size) of this mixture add half a cup of bone meal or superphosphate, half a cup of general fertiliser like SR 3:1:5 (26) and a level tablespoon of agricultural lime.

## Planting

1. Before planting, remember to wash out the container. If it is of a porous material, soak it well before filling with moist potting mix. This will prevent the container walls from absorbing moisture from the potting mix, which will cause the potting mix to shrink away from the sides of the container and leave a gap where water will run off when the plant is watered, leaving the centre of the potting mix dry.
2. There must be enough drainage holes – at least four to five 1-cm holes in a pot of 45 cm in diameter.
3. Cover drainage holes with a single piece of broken terracotta (crock) or use a piece of gauze or shade cloth.
4. Add a layer of river sand, about 3 cm thick, over this to prevent holes from becoming blocked up and to act as a filter to prevent compost material and soil from washing out. Do not add too much sand to small containers as it will only take up valuable potting-mix space. Rather use a piece of gauze.
5. Add moisture-retaining granules to the potting mix.
6. Water the plant well before planting it out into your container.
7. Fill the container with potting mix to accommodate the root ball of the plant. Remove the plant from its bag or pot, fit it carefully into the container, fill up with potting mix around the root ball and firm down. Leave a space of about 5 cm below the rim to make watering easier.
8. Add a layer of compost to act as mulch, or plant colourful annuals to serve as living mulch. Decorative pebbles or chips of pine bark also lend an attractive finish.
9. Water well.

Some outdoor plants that come from a greenhouse or shaded area need to be kept in the shade for a while after being planted. Move them to direct sunlight in stages, in order to prevent the foliage from getting sunburned.

These pots with daisy bushes, strikingly positioned at different levels, make a bold statement.

## Watering and feeding

Watering is the most important factor in keeping container plants healthy. In the hot summer months containers in full sun will need daily attention, especially if containers are made from porous material like terracotta or concrete. A good general rule is to water containers well and allow excess water to flow out of drainage holes. It will only be necessary to water again once the top 6–7 cm of the potting mix is beginning to dry out. There is no hard-and-fast rule for when to water; it depends entirely on the position of the container and the climatic conditions.

It is important to remember that certain nutrients will be leached from the potting mix with excess water through the drainage holes. Fertilise with liquid fertiliser every two weeks throughout the active growing season in summer. Never fertilise plants if the potting mix is dry, as plants can suffer from root burn. Always feed after a good watering. It is also very convenient to use appropriate plant-food sticks with slow-release nitrogen.

## Pruning

Many foliage and flowering plants need trimming and shaping, especially standard shrubs and trees. Pinch back new shoots regularly to promote bushier growth. A third of the top growth can be removed from plants that require winter pruning.

## Repotting

It will be necessary to repot a container plant once roots start to protrude from drainage holes or growth becomes stunted and the plant doesn't flower as it should. When transplanting a plant from one pot to another, make sure that the next pot or container is just one size larger and not too big, so that the plant and the container still look in proportion and not overpotted.

You might want to use the same container for a plant of which the growth has been stunted because of restricted root space. The plant will need repotting after a few years to keep it in good condition, and this can be done during winter. Remove the plant from the container and wash the container well on the inside as well as the outside. Shave off a few centimetres of the root ball and return it to the container with fresh potting mix. You can also trim and shape the plant at the same time.

## Plants for outdoor containers

You can grow almost any plant in a container, provided it gets enough water and nutrients. A further advantage of containers is that plants with invasive growing habits, for instance bamboo, can be grown in them. Trees with a slow growth habit are very good for containers, as they will not become root-bound too quickly. Conifers and slow-growing deciduous trees are very good examples. You also have the advantage of growing shrubs like azaleas, camellias and hydrangeas very successfully in containers, as you can provide the acid potting mix that they prefer. Many shrubs with scented flowers can also be grown in this way and brought to the patio to be enjoyed when they are in full flower. Roses are a good example. Many varieties are suitable to grow in containers and a standard rose with annuals around the base can provide a splash of colour throughout summer and the rest of the year.

Annuals and herbs are excellent grouped around the base of larger plants in containers or on their own in shallow bowls or window boxes. Bulbs are also a good choice for providing colour in containers. Even vegetables can be grown in containers as long as the container depth is not less than 24 cm. Strawberries are the easiest fruit to grow in pots, especially in containers with special openings on the sides.

Listed below are some recommended trees and shrubs suitable for containers:

**Trees:** *Acer palmatum* and cultivars (Japanese maples), *Citrus* spp., *Chrysalidocarpus lutescens* (yellow bamboo palm), \**Cunonia capensis* (red alder), \**Euphorbia ingens* (common tree euphorbia), *Ficus benjamina* (weeping fig), \**Halleria lucida* (tree fuchsia), *Livistona chinensis* (Chinese fan palm), *Magnolia grandiflora* (laurel magnolia), \**Nuxia floribunda* (forest elder), *Trachycarpus fortunei* (Chinese windmill palm).

**Shrubs:** *Abelia grandiflora* 'Francis Mason', \**Anisodontea* 'Lady's Pink' (mallow), *Ardisia crispa* (coral-berry tree), *Aucuba japonica* (spotted laurel), azaleas, *Beaucarnea recurvata* (pony-tail palm), *Callistemon* 'Little John', camellias, *Codiaeum variegatum* (croton), conifers, coprosma, *Cycas revoluta* (sago palm), \**Dracaena alteriformis* (large-leaved dragon tree), *Duranta* 'Sheena's Gold', \**Encephalartos* spp. (cycads), *Fatsia japonica* (Japanese fatsia), *Fuchsia* hybrids, *Gardenia* varieties, *Hibiscus rosa-sinensis* (Chinese hibiscus), hydrangeas, *Kalanchoe beharensis* (velvet bush), *Laurus nobilis* (bay laurel), *Murraya exotica* (orange jessamine), *Myrtus communis* (myrtle), *Nandina domestica* (sacred bamboo), \**Ochna serrulata* (plane bush), *Philodendron selloum* (split-leaved philodendron), *Philodendron* 'Xanadu', *Phoenix roebelenii* (dwarf date palm), *Phormium* varieties (flax), \**Plumbago auriculata* (blue plumbago), \**Portulacaria afra* (spekboom), *Rosa sinensis* (roses), *Rosmarinus officinalis* (rosemary), *Schefflera* varieties, *Solanum rantonetti* (blue potato bush), *Syzygium paniculatum* 'Globulum' (dwarf eugenia), *Trachelospermum jasminoides* 'Chameleon', *Yucca flaccida* 'Garland Gold' (Spanish sword).

## Questions and answers

**Q: Is it a good idea to encourage earthworms in container plants?**

A: Earthworms are very good in the open ground but do quite a lot of damage if they are encouraged in containers. The constant burrowing of the earthworms disturbs the root system and disrupts the drainage material to such an extent that the drainage holes get blocked. It is easy to rid container plants of earthworms: simply water the potting mix with a solution of half a teaspoon of permanganate of potash (Condy's crystals) to one litre of water. It will not harm the plants but will cause the worms to wriggle to the surface immediately.

**Q: Could you give me some ideas of how and where to use different types of containers?**

A group of different-sized pots make an entrance feature with a standard bay (*Laurus nobilis*), purple flax (*Phormium tenax* 'Atropurpurea') and *Euonymus japonicus* 'Microphyllus' as the central attractions.

A: In an indigenous garden, use ethnic pots, either in a group of three or singly as a focal point.

- To display plants with bold foliage, try to use plain containers of the same shape and colour and different sizes.
- Use identical containers with identical plants to create an elegant effect at an entrance, for example.
- Very elaborate pots that are grouped together should all be in the same style and planted up with plain green plants that will not compete with the container.
- If pots are all different in style and used together, paint them the same colour.
- Shallow, bowl-type containers and troughs are well suited to a cottage garden theme.
- A very large, empty container can be used to great effect as a focal point in a gravel garden, for example.
- For a very hot north- or west-facing patio, use water-wise succulents of contrasting colours, shapes and sizes to give a sculptured effect.
- Colourful glazed or terracotta containers look good in a Mediterranean- or Provençal-style garden.
- Wooden barrels, embossed white containers and urns suit English-style gardens.
- Glazed pots look good in Oriental-style gardens.

**Q: I have been told to use charcoal in the bottom of my pots. What is the reason for this?**

A: A layer of charcoal in the bottom of the container helps to keep the soil near to neutral and prevents it from becoming too acid.

**Q: What is the best way to remove a plant that needs repotting from a container with an opening narrower than its middle or base section, without breaking the container?**

A: 1. Water the plant well and let the container lie on its side.

2. Use a hose with high-pressure water and wash out the potting mix, starting from the sides towards the middle.

3. Once the potting mix is washed out the roots will be flexible so that the plant can be pulled out of the container.

4. The plant can now be trimmed and replanted, either into the garden or into a larger container.

5. The base of an old, broken lawnmower is ideal for manoeuvring large containers around.

**Q: I live in a townhouse and have very limited space. How can I have a colourful display throughout the year, as well as foliage shrubs and trees ?**

A: Most plants can be grown in containers as long as the container is large enough for the particular plant. Choose evergreen trees or standard flowering shrubs with annuals around the base for colour. Annuals can be changed as the seasons change, and you will have the advantage of combining very interesting colour combinations for a colourful effect. It is also a good idea to grow creepers in containers against a trellis in restricted areas. Some colourful creepers to consider would be *Bougainvillea* 'Tropical Rainbow', clematis, *Gelsemium sempervirens* (Carolina jasmine), *Mandevilla amoena* 'Alice du Pont' (pink dipladenia), *Mandevilla boliviensis* (white dipladenia), *Pandorea jasminoides* varieties (bower plant), *Stephanotis floribunda* (Madagascar jasmine), *Trachelospermum jasminoides* (star jasmine), *Vigna caracalla* (snail vine).

### Q: How large should a container for a small tree be?
A: The larger the better. Small containers dry out too fast in summer and roots may get damaged during cold winters. Do not choose a container smaller than at least 50 cm in diameter.

### Q: Which plants can be grown in window boxes and troughs?
A: Most annuals, bulbs, herbs and many perennials would be suitable for container culture.

### Q: Can you give me some information on which fruit trees to grow in containers?
A: Most dwarf citrus trees like calamondin, kumquat, clementine and Meyer lemons are very ornamental and will provide fruit if the container is large enough. If you want prolific, fruit-bearing plants it would be better to grow fruit trees in the open ground. Strawberries are also easy to grow in containers.

### Q: Is it possible to grow palms on the patio? We experience heavy frost in our area.
A: Most palms are either too large or too tender to grow in containers in your area. You can grow the European fan palm (*Chamaerops humilis*) very successfully in a container, however, as it is hardy and slow-growing. *Trachycarpus fortunei* (Chinese windmill palm) is also a good choice.

### Q: How does one successfully grow roses in containers?
A: It is important to remember that the container size relates to the plant growth habit: the bigger the plant, the bigger the container. Young plants can be started in smaller containers and eventually repotted as it becomes necessary. Roses need at least six hours of direct sun per day, preferably morning sun. The best time to plant a rose out of the open ground into a container would be in late winter. Roses grown in plastic bags or pots and bought from a nursery can be planted up any time of the year. Prepare a good, soil-based potting mix by mixing 70% prepared potting soil with 20% good garden loam and 10% coarse river sand. Fill the container and water well to let the soil settle in the container. Leave the pot overnight. Before potting a rose from the open ground, prune the plant hard and cut back the roots as well. Plant the rose in the container. Water well and feed regularly during the active growing season. The art of keeping roses happy in containers is to water and feed them correctly. Roses grown in containers need more care and attention than those grown in the open ground.

### Q: What does 'overpotted' mean?
A: An overpotted plant is a young plant that is not mature yet and has been planted in too large a container. A young plant started from seed or a cutting needs to be planted into a small container that is in proportion to its size. Young plants do not yet have a very well-developed root system and cannot cope with too much moisture and plant food in containers that are too large for its size.

# indoor plants

As the pace of life accelerates, with ever-increasing demands and pressures on our daily lives, a restful atmosphere in our homes becomes essential. Plants in the home provide such an atmosphere. The range of indoor plants is very accommodating – there is a suitable plant for nearly any situation in the home. Plants and containers of all conceivable shapes, sizes and colours offer you endless opportunities to enhance the decor of your home.

Indoor plants are plants that can adapt to indoor growing conditions. Most of these are from tropical rainforests, where they grow in the shade of large trees in a warm and humid atmosphere. When growing indoor plants, one should keep this in mind and try to duplicate these conditions. There are, however, many plants from dry regions as well, like succulents that do just as well indoors.

## Choice of plants

It is often difficult for some people to decide what plant to buy. They should first of all consider the suitability of the plant for the purpose it is intended for, and then choose a healthy, well-grown specimen that will last if well cared for.

Listed below are some basic rules to keep in mind when buying and choosing indoor plants:

- Always buy indoor plants from a reputable garden centre, nursery or shop, because these plants will be well hardened off (acclimatised) for growing in the home.
- Do not buy plants with roots growing out of drainage holes, as these will already be pot-bound.
- The plant should be compact and leaves should just overlap the rim of the pot. Tall and slim plants should be at least twice the height of the pot.
- Flowering plants should have 50% closed buds, otherwise the display of plants in full flower will soon be over.
- Avoid plants with signs of pests and diseases and green mould on the surface of the potting soil.
- Do not buy plants that are not clearly identified or named.

## Plant requirements

### Light

All plants need light to grow. Plants from different parts of the world vary enormously in their need for light. A good way to determine if enough light is available, is to hold one's hand against a sheet of white paper: if a shadow is cast, there is enough light for most indoor plants. The duration of natural light or strong artificial light should be 12 to 16 hours to maintain active growth.

African violets, one of the best-known and most popular flowering indoor plants.

*Nephrolepis exaltata* 'Tuffii', a variety of the well-known sword fern (top); and *Aglaonema commutatum*, an excellent choice for any home (bottom).

Plants with variegated foliage need more light than green-foliaged plants. Flowering plants need some direct sunlight, and succulents and cacti have the highest light requirements. There are, however, some exceptions to these rules.

The following is a general list of plants for different light situations:

**Low-light situations:** *Aspidistra elatior* (cast-iron plant), *Aglaonema commutatum* (Chinese evergreen), *Rhoicissus rhomboidea* (grape ivy), *Fatsia japonica* (Japanese fatsia), *Fatshedera lizei* (tree ivy), *Philodendron scandens* (sweetheart plant) and Kentia palm.

**Medium-light situations:** *Ardisia crenata* (coral berry), bromeliads, cyclamen, *Dieffenbachia amoena* (dumb cane), *Chamaedorea* palm varieties, *Scindapsus aureus* (devil's ivy), *Spathiphyllum wallisii* (peace lily), *Schefflera* varieties (parasol plant and umbrella tree), *Aralia* (false aralia) and *Philodendron* varieties.

**Bright light but not direct sunlight:** Flowering plants, succulents and cacti, croton, ferns and *Ficus* varieties.

## Temperature

Indoor plants need a fairly constant temperature of about 20 °C in the active growing season, with a lower temperature during winter. Plants are quite tolerant of normal fluctuations in day and night temperatures. Avoid temperature extremes, as these can be fatal or cause damage.

## Water

Each plant has its own basic need of water, which depends on the size of the plant, the size of the container, the potting mix, the season and the environment. Watering can therefore never become a regular routine. A good way to determine when to water is by looking at and feeling the surface. Water when the surface is dry and powdery all over. Exceptions are cacti and succulents, which need much less water. Water should never stand in the drip tray for more than a day, as this will cause waterlogging. Remember, all plants need less water in winter as it is their resting period. More pot plants die from overwatering than from any pot plant pest or disease.

## Humidity

The amount of moisture in the air determines the humidity. Most indoor plants need a higher humidity than is normal in a lounge or living room. By grouping plants together a humid microclimate is created by the foliage and increased moisture from damp potting mixes. Heated and air-conditioned rooms have very low humidity and misting plants will be necessary. Misting the leaves will also help to discourage red spider mite and will reduce dust on leaves. One can also use pebble trays, where the pot plants are stood on top of a tray filled with small pebbles or gravel and water.

## Cultivation

### Potting mix

The best potting mix for indoor plants is one that holds moisture but is also well aerated, free-draining and rich in plant food. Ready-made potting soil mixes fulfil these needs and can be bought in bags. It is possible, however, to make one's own potting mix by mixing three parts good garden loam, two parts well-rotted compost or peat moss and one part coarse sand. To each 10-litre bucketful of this mix, add a handful of bone meal and a handful of a general fertiliser like Wonder Planting and Vegetables 2:3:4 (21) + 30% Lime.

### Repotting

Pot plants only need to be repotted once they are pot-bound. A plant is pot-bound when it grows very slowly, even with regular feeding, when the potting mix dries out very quickly and when roots grow out of the drainage holes. If the plant is removed carefully, one will notice a matted mass of roots on the outside with little potting mix visible.

1. Use a pot only one size larger to avoid overpotting. Make sure that the pot is clean and cover the drainage holes with broken pieces of crock – one per hole is all that is necessary. Coarse river sand can also be used.
2. Cover with a shallow layer of potting mix.
3. Remove the pot-bound plant, which has been well watered previously, and loosen some of the outside matted roots.
4. Place on top of the potting-mix layer in the new pot and fill around the root ball with potting mix.
5. Press down the potting mix and make sure that the level of the base of the stem is about 2 cm below the rim of the pot. Water well and treat the plant normally.

Some large pot plants can be revitalised, without being repotted, through top-dressing. This needs to be done in spring by removing the top 5-cm layer of potting mix and replacing it with fresh potting mix.

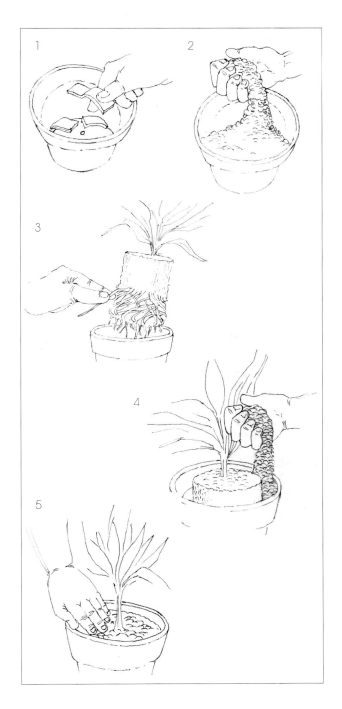

## Feeding

Pot plants need to be fed regularly in their active growing season, usually from spring to autumn. This is necessary because the potting mix contains only a limited amount of plant food, which is continually depleted by leaching and by the roots of the growing plant. The amount of fertiliser needed will depend on the size of the plant and that of the container. Follow the instructions on the plant-food container to avoid overfeeding. There are many different pot plant fertilisers available, from powder-type plant foods to liquid concentrates and plant-food sticks with slow-release nitrogen. The most effective way to feed your plants would be to use liquid fertiliser diluted in water, so that feeding and watering are done in one operation.

## Pests and diseases

Pot plants will become susceptible to pests and diseases as soon as they are under stress, for example if they are under- or overfed, under- or overwatered or deprived of sufficient light.

**Aphids:** Small, sap-sucking insects, usually green or black, occurring on new-growth tips and flower buds. They cause distorted leaves. Spray with Aphicide or Baysol as a foliar spray or use Insecticide Granules applied to the potting mix. A general-purpose aerosol insecticide, such as Garden Gun or Natural Insecticide Concentrate, can be used for quicker results. Alternatively, spray with soapy water.

**Mealybug:** White, cottony insects on the undersides of leaves and on stems. If only a few are present, wipe them off with a damp cloth. A heavy infestation will have to be sprayed with either Aphicide, Baysol, Chlorpirifos, Dursban 2E, Garden Gun, Garden Ripcord, Malasol, Malathion or Natural Insecticide.

**Scale insects:** Round, flattened, reddish, brown or grey insects on stems and leaves. They suck sap of plants, causing growth to be retarded. Spray with Chlorpirifos, Dursban 2E, Folithion, Garden Gun, Malasol, Malathion or Oleum. Soapy water (5 ml of dishwashing liquid in 1 litre of water) can also be used, whereafter insects can be wiped off with a damp cloth.

**Mites:** Minute, sap-sucking, eight-legged creatures on the undersides of leaves, appearing under hot and dry conditions. Leaves become speckled and silvery-pale and there may also be spider webbing present. They cause leaves to drop. Spray with Chlorpirifos, Garden Gun, Malathion, Redspidercide or Redspiderspray.

**Whitefly:** Small, winged insect, covered with white powder and found on the undersides of leaves. They suck sap and cause retarded growth. Spray with Natural Insecticide, Garden Gun, Garden Ripcord or Whitefly Insecticide.

**Root rot:** A soil-borne fungus disease which causes yellowing and wilting of leaves, followed by collapse. Poor drainage and overwatering usually cause the disease to appear. Treat with Fongarid.

**Sooty mould:** A black fungus growing on honeydew, which is a secondary infection following the presence of aphids, mealybug, scale or whitefly. Spray with soapy water (5 ml dishwashing liquid in 1 litre of water) and wipe with a damp cloth. Control the insect pest causing the problem.

## Questions and answers

**Q: How do I go about cleaning the foliage of my pot plants?**

A: Plants with hairy foliage like African violets, succulents and cacti should be brushed with a soft brush. Small plants with smooth leaves can be rinsed under a hand shower: hold the pot at an angle and rinse gently with tepid water. You can do this with your African violets as well, but make sure that the leaves dry off quickly. Large plants have to be sponged and wiped with a damp cloth. Remember to support the leaves with your hand while wiping. Do not use oil as a leaf shine, as it clogs the pores in the leaves and collects dust. Only use a product that has been specially made for plants.

**Q: I have a beautiful, large *Ficus benjamina* which has been losing its leaves since I moved to another house. They turn yellow and fall. What can be the problem?**

A: Well-established, large plants tend to resent moving, especially some of the many different *Ficus* varieties. Leaves turn yellow and fall as a result of either a change in temperature, overwatering or a draught in the new position. If there is sufficient light available you will have to let the plant acclimatise to its new position by leaving it there without moving it again, making sure that the problem wasn't caused by a draught. Only if there is a draught should the plant be moved again to a better position. Water only when the surface of the potting mix is dry and do not overwater.

**Q: The leaves of my variegated pot plant are turning green. What can I do to prevent this from happening?**

A: This is usually caused by the leaves not receiving sufficient light. The plant will have to be moved to a brighter position. If only a portion of the plant is green and the rest variegated, then carefully cut out the part with the green leaves.

**Q: The tips of my bamboo palm are turning brown. What is causing this problem?**

A: If the tips go brown and leaf edges remain green, the cause is usually dry air. This can be prevented by increasing the humidity: place the palm in a drip tray filled with pebbles and water, or use a mist sprayer regularly. Overwatering or extreme cases of drying out, on the other hand, can also cause similar symptoms.

**Q: I have a rubber plant which has become too big for the house. Can it be planted into the garden?**

A: This is really not a good idea, as the rubber tree has an invasive root system which will damage paving and underground pipes and lift walls. It is not a garden-friendly plant for South African gardens! Overgrown pot plants should be discarded if a suitable position in the garden cannot be found for them. Most suburban gardens are too small for rubber trees.

**Q: I have been given a bromeliad. How do I care for it?**

A: Bromeliads are tropical plants and need high temperatures to flower. They require bright light and a high humidity in summer. Water them into the central rosette or vase rather than into the potting mix, which has to be kept

A variegated *Ficus benjamina* growing well in an indoor courtyard with good light.

*Cyclamen persicum* is available in a range of lovely whites, lilacs, pinks and brilliant reds.

moist as well. The parent rosette that has finished flowering will die down and must be removed. Offsets appear at the base of plants and can be removed to make new plants. Repotting is usually not necessary. Bromeliads thrive in rather small pots and a very friable, loose potting mixture.

### Q: Why does my anthurium no longer flower?

A: Anthuriums need warm temperatures, especially during winter, and bright light without direct sunlight. They do not flower if the humidity is too low. Keep the potting mix moist at all times and mist the foliage regularly. The potting mixture should also be very friable and porous. In addition, you can surround the pot with moist peat moss to help keep the humidity high.

### Q: I have a variegated *Monstera deliciosa* (delicious monster) which develops dry patches on the leaves. The moisture level is checked with a meter before watering. What can be the cause of this problem?

A: The dry patches on the foliage are usually an indication of cold and low-light conditions. Move the plant to a warmer position, out of a draught, and where there is brighter daylight available. Variegated plants always need more light than their green family members.

### Q: My African violets are situated in front of an east-facing window, protected by an awning. They have always done very well but are suddenly droopy and sad-looking.

A: The most common cause of sad-looking African violets is overwatering. It can also be the result of crown rot, which is caused by poor ventilation, too-wet potting soil, sudden changes in temperature and a potting mix that does not drain well. The best treatment would be to remove wilted leaves and not to overwater or get the crown of the plant wet. Treat with Fongarid. It might be a good idea to start new plants from healthy leaves and discard old ones, as they seldom recover sufficiently.

### Q: How can I successfully grow a staghorn fern?

A: *Platycerium bifurcatum* or the staghorn fern is an epiphyte, which means that it lives off the compost that collects behind the 'shield' that develops behind the staghorn-like fronds. The best way to grow these ferns would be to attach them to a piece of bark or rough wood. Do this by putting peat moss or leaf mould on the bark and place the fern with its 'shield' onto this. Secure everything onto the piece of bark or wood with a nylon stocking or nylon twine. This can now be hung in or secured onto a tree or against a cool wall in the shade. Water regularly during the hot and dry weather and feed with liquid plant food like Nitrosol or Baby Bio once a month during the summer months.

**Q: When is the best time to divide and replant old Boston ferns (*Nephrolepis exaltata*)?**

A: In early spring, choose young and stronger crowns from the outer perimeter of the plant to replant, and discard old, woody crowns from the centre. Do not remove air roots and use a well-drained, organic potting mix. Keep the potting mix moist but not soggy.

**Q: What are the best ferns for keeping indoors?**

A: Different types of Boston ferns, bird's-nest ferns, Pteris ferns, holly ferns and rabbit's-foot ferns. All these should do well in medium- to bright-light situations, if reasonably looked after.

**Q: How does one plant an amaryllis bulb for pot culture?**

A: Use a pot large enough to hold the bulb, with 1 cm of space between the bulb and the rim of the pot. Plant in potting mix with the top half of the bulb exposed, and water from the bottom. Do this from July to October. Water and feed while leaves are developing and present in spring and summer. Keep dry when leaves have died down and repot every third year.

**Q: Which plants would be suitable to grow in a terrarium?**

A: Various small ferns, selaginella, begonias, small ivies, pileas, fittonias, maranta, peperomia and any plants that appreciate very humid conditions.

**Q: I have been given a beautiful *Kalanchoe blossfeldiana* in flower, but the leaves have been dropping since I brought it indoors.**

A: This is usually caused by a sudden change in environmental conditions and, particularly, in humidity. The interior of the house is probably much drier than the hothouse where the plant was grown. Keep the potting mix moist and mist-spray the foliage on hot days.

**Q: How does one grow cyclamen successfully indoors?**

A: Cyclamen like a cool and humid atmosphere, away from too much sunlight. Water when the surface of the potting mix feels dry. Move them at night to a colder area in the home. They should flower for at least three months. Remove faded blooms and yellowing leaves regularly. After blooming, gradually dry off the plant and rest it in a cool, dry place.

**Q: Could you please tell me how and when to divide cymbidium orchids?**

A: Cymbidiums do not need to be broken up too often, as flowering will be affected. Divide overgrown pots when the plants are no longer growing vigorously and look stunted. The best time to divide them would be in late summer. Soak the whole plant well before turning it out of its container. When dividing, be sure to untangle the roots carefully so that each division has at least three mature 'pseudobulbs' with leaves. Bulbs without leaves can be potted up in separate, smaller pots. Before replanting, shorten the roots by removing about one-third of the root length. Make sure that the fresh potting medium (rock wool, bark chips or marble chips) is settled well around the roots, with at least two-thirds of the 'pseudobulb' showing above the medium. Water well and keep in a shady area for the first few weeks to settle down. Never allow the medium to dry out completely.

# invaders
# and weeds

## Invaders

Invaders are alien plants that have become invasive by replacing the natural vegetation. Many of these invaders were useful as decorative plants in home gardens, or were introduced to South Africa as plantation crops or for stabilising sand dunes and have now spread beyond their bounds. Invaders have become naturalised in many areas of our landscape and are posing a very real danger in that they choke rivers, dams and irrigation channels and reduce available water for indigenous plants and wildlife. They have very competitive root systems and canopies, thereby replacing natural vegetation, which upsets the ecological balance. They also disfigure scenery and transform very nutritious grazing and cropland into wasteland because the natural ecosystem has been destroyed. Many indigenous insect species that were dependent on the natural vegetation, are lost, which in turn causes birds, mammals and reptiles dependent on these insects to disappear as well. Dense thickets of plant invaders in catchment areas also increase the threat of fires. Plant invaders have become very successful because they have no natural enemies like insects and diseases to hold them in check, whereas indigenous species must survive with competition from aliens and many natural enemies like insects, diseases and animals.

It is very important to know and recognise plant invaders in order to help control their spread. Plants that have been declared noxious weeds by law cannot be grown anywhere in the country. It is the duty of all South Africans to destroy invaders in their gardens or on their land.

Listed below are some very well-known invaders that were introduced as garden plants:

Bugtree (*Solanum mauritianum*) is a noxious weed introduced from South America. It is a very fast-growing small tree which can grow up to 10 m high. Foliage is covered in velvety hairs; purple flowers appear throughout the year with yellow fruits, which are poisonous and contain many seeds. Seeds can lie dormant for ten years and are dispersed mostly by birds. It is also a breeding ground for fruitfly. Control by pulling out seedlings manually, or use a herbicide like Roundup as a foliar spray for shrub-sized bushes, or use Garlon 4 to treat stumps of larger plants.

Lantana (*Lantana camara*). This noxious weed is from South and Central America. It is an evergreen shrub which can reach a height of about 3 m. Flowers appear in compact heads and colours range from white, pink, red, orange and yellow to combinations of these colours. They are followed by very poisonous green berries which turn dark purple when ripe. Birds distribute seeds. Control by destroying seedlings or use a herbicide like Garlon 4 as a stump treatment or Ridder/Roundup as foliar spray treatment.

*Lantana camara*, a noxious weed from South and Central America.

Although beautiful, cat's-claw creeper (*Macfadyena unguis-cati*) is a noxious weed which is lethal in the garden as it is extremely invasive and smothers other plants and buildings.

Seringa (*Melia azedarach*) is a fast-growing, large deciduous tree from Asia. It bears clusters of fragrant, pale-mauve flowers in spring, followed by drooping sprays of poisonous, yellow or brownish fruits. Birds disperse fruits. Control by destroying seedlings or kill trees with herbicide like Garlon 4 as a stump treatment, or ring-bark mature trees.

Pampas grass (*Cortaderia selloana*), a large, fast-growing, clump-forming grass with white to pink plumes and abrasive foliage, is native to Argentina. It is a garden plant and also used in Gauteng for erosion control on mine dumps. Control it by burning it down to the ground to guard against further seeding.

Brazilian glory pea (*Sesbania punicea*) is a deciduous small tree or shrub from South America. It has drooping, compound leaves and showy red or orange flowers in spring, followed by four-winged seed pods which are dispersed by water. Flowers and seeds are poisonous. Control by cutting bushes as low as possible.

Cat's-claw creeper (*Macfadyena unguis-cati*) is a fast-growing tendril climber from tropical America. It is semideciduous and bears yellow, trumpet-like flowers in spring and early summer. It produces many papery seeds which are wind-dispersed. It is very difficult to eradicate its fleshy roots. Biological control by means of a beetle which is its natural enemy, seems to be the only means of controlling this invasive creeper.

Blackwood (*Acacia melanoxylon*) is an evergreen, upright-growing tree with a dense crown originating from Australia. It is fast-growing and has been grown for furniture timber. Creamy-white flowers appear in spring, followed by brown seed pods. Seeds are black and can remain in the soil for decades before germinating. Trees also spread by means of root suckers. Control by eradicating all seedlings and ring-barking mature trees.

Queen of the night (*Cereus peruvianus*) is a South American cactus with large, white flowers. Seeds are dispersed by birds and monkeys. It is a noxious weed. Control by burning or spraying with herbicide.

Water hyacinth (*Eichhornia crassipes*) is a water plant native to South America. It is free-floating or mud-rooted with a rosette of leaves with swollen, bladder-like stalks and pale violet flower spikes during summer. It spreads very quickly by means of side shoots that break off and become separate plants. Control this weed mechanically by removing plants from the water. They can also be chemically controlled by means of herbicide treatment.

The following is a list of more invader plants to guard against: *Acacia cyclops* (rooikrans), *A. dealbata* (silver wattle), *A. decurrens* (green wattle), *A. longifolia* (long-leaved wattle), *A. mearnsii* (black wattle), *A. pycnantha* (golden wattle), *A. saligna* (Port Jackson willow), *Agave sisalana* (sisal), *Albizia lophantha* (Australian false thorn), *Araujia sericifera* (moth catcher), *Arundo donax* (Spanish reed), *Caesalpinia decapetala* (Mauritius thorn), *Chromolaena odorata* (triffid weed), *Hakea gibbosa* (rock hakea), *H. sericea* (silky hakea), *H. suaveolens* (sweet hakea), *Hypericum perforatum* (St. John's wort), *Ipomoea alba* (moonflower), *Jacaranda mimosifolia* (jacaranda), *Leptospermum laevigatum* (Australian myrtle), *Ligustrum* varieties (all non-grafted privets), *Nerium oleander* (all single-flowering varieties), *Nicotiana glauca* (wild tobacco), *Opuntia aurantiaca* (jointed cactus), *O. ficus-indica* (sweet prickly pear), *O. imbricata* (chain-link cactus), *O. rosea* (rosea cactus), *Pinus patula* (patula pine), *P. pinaster* (cluster pine), *Pistia stratiotes* (water lettuce), *Prosopis glandulosa* (mesquite), *Pyracantha angustifolia* (yellow fire-thorn), *Populus canescens* (grey poplar), *Psidium guajava* (guava), *Ricinus communis* (castor oil plant), *Rubus* spp. (bramble), *Salix babylonica* (weeping willow), *Salvinia molesta* (Kariba weed) and *Stipa trichotoma* (nassella tussock grass).

Alien invader plants owe their success to their ability to grow vigorously, their massive seed production, their ability to sprout again after felling and their unpalatability to indigenous insects and animals.

## Invader control

The control of plant invaders is not easy and involves various methods suitable for different species. Methods of control are:

- Chemical control with herbicides. It is not always possible to use herbicides in cases where selective plant control is needed or the prevention of environmental pollution is a priority.
- Mechanical control involves the slashing, cutting or stumping, burial or removal of plants by means of burning, ploughing and deforestation.
- Biological control is the introduction of their own natural enemies to help control the spread of invaders. It is not always possible, however, to introduce a natural enemy of an invader, because it may also attack useful indigenous plants or may not be effective in the new environment.
- Ring-barking is a very effective and easy method to kill many woody plants.

# Weeds

Weeds are herbaceous plants that grow very well, but are unwanted, in cultivated places and disturbed soil.

## Weed control

Most weeds are easy to control through regular hand-weeding, hoeing or shallow cultivation before they reach flowering stage, to prevent them from seeding themselves again. 'One year's seeding is seven years' weeding' is a well-known saying that holds true for most weeds. Ground-cover plants can also be used to form a living carpet to suppress weeds, while acting as a live mulch.

Severe weed infestations can also be controlled with herbicides or weedkillers. There are two main types of weedkillers – selective and nonselective. Selective weedkillers are used to kill either broad-leaved or grass-like weeds. Nonselective weedkillers will kill only green plants and cannot be translocated through the plant if administered to brown bark or wood. They immediately break down in the soil.

For controlling weeds with weedkillers a knapsack sprayer or a pressurised garden sprayer must be used. Spray equipment used for weedkillers should never be used to spray pesticides or liquid plant foods afterwards, as sensitive plants like roses may suffer from small amounts of weedkiller left over in the spray equipment.

When using weedkillers, care must be taken to avoid spray drifting onto flowers, shrubs and trees, which will also be susceptible to the weedkiller. Never spray weedkillers on a windy day. Always spray in the early morning when the soil is moist, and avoid spraying in the heat of the day. Weedkiller needs at least six hours of dry weather to be effective. If rain occurs within six hours, the application will have to be repeated. Always use protective clothing and follow instructions carefully. Never exceed the recommended dosage rate.

## Weeds in lawns

Broad-leaved weeds in lawns can easily be eradicated, without killing the lawn, by spraying with a selective weedkiller. Selective weedkillers are usually used on lawns to kill broad-leaved weeds like creeping sorrel, clover, dandelion, creeping milkweed, purslane and devil's thorn. These weeds can be controlled selectively with either Banweed M.C.P.A., Hormoban or Turfweeder. If there was a heavy infestation of weeds a second application after three to four weeks will be necessary. The active ingredients in the formulations are only effective in the soil for two to four weeks. These weedkillers should never be used in flowerbeds or amongst roses. Winter grass (*Poa annua*) usually occurs in shady, moist areas during winter and can be controlled with Kerb. This weedkiller can be used on lawns of the *Cynodon* type and on Kikuyu. It cannot be applied to Outeniqua lawn varieties. Where yellow nutgrass is a problem, use Basagran while plants are still actively growing.

It is recommended that the lawn be fed – two to three weeks before applying weedkiller –with a fertiliser high in nitrogen, for example Wonder Lawn and Foliage 7:1:3 (21) or 3:2:1 (28) SR. This will promote active lawn and weed growth for optimum results with the weedkiller. The lawn will also be able to withstand treatment better.

## Weeds in paved areas

All weeds in paved areas can easily be eradicated with a nonselective weedkiller like Roundup, Ridder or Paving Weed Killer. Always spray onto the green parts to ensure effective control. It may take four days to two weeks for weeds to die, depending on the type of weed. Pouring boiling salted water on weeds in paved areas will also kill them and curb regrowth.

## Weeds in flowerbeds

In prepared flowerbeds or vegetable beds where there is a severe weed infestation Roundup or Ridder can be used as a spray before planting. These weedkillers have no residual effect on the soil and will not affect animals. Amongst flowers, however, Roundup or Ridder will have to be used very carefully as a spot treatment directly onto weeds. Broad-leaved weeds cannot be sprayed if shrubs and other broad-leaved plants surround them, as these will also be killed. If herbicide treatment is not an option, shallow cultivation or hand-weeding can be done early on a hot day. Leave weeds lying on top of the soil to dry out. A thick mulch of coarse, organic material will also help to smother weeds. Black plastic sheeting can be used in the vegetable garden to control weeds.

The following herbicides can be used for the most common broad-leaved weeds as a spot treatment in flowerbeds:

**Banweed:** for blackjack (*Bidens pilosa*), khaki weed (*Tagetes minuta*) and on new lawns.

**Hormoban:** for Mexican poppy (*Argemone* spp.), creeping sorrel (*Oxalis corniculata*), blackjack (*Bidens pilosa*), flax-leaf fleabane (*Conyza* or *Erigeron bonariensis*), devil's thorn (*Tribulus terrestris*), sow thistle (*Sonchus oleraceus*), purslane (*Portulaca oleracea*), creeping milkweed (*Euphorbia inaequilatera*) and on existing lawns.

**Turfweeder:** for Mexican poppy (*Argemone* spp.), creeping sorrel (*Oxalis corniculata*), devil's thorn (*Tribulus ter-

*restris*), sow thistle (*Sonchus oleraceus*), purslane (*Portulaca oleracea*) and creeping milkweed (*Euphorbia inaequilatera*) and on existing lawns.
**Roundup/Ridder:** for small-flowered quickweed (*Galinsoga parviflora*) and all other broad-leaved weeds.

## Questions and answers

### Q: I have onionweed in my garden. How can I get rid of this pest?
A: Onionweed, also known as wild garlic (*Nothoscordum inodorum*), originally came from North America and has become very invasive in recent years. The best way to eradicate it is to dig it out by hand to ensure that all the little bulbs surrounding the mother plant are lifted and destroyed. Be careful not to lose any of these small bulbs, as they will grow again. You can also spot-treat plants by painting Roundup or Ridder directly onto the foliage. It is important that plants are never allowed to reach flowering stage, to curb them from spreading further.

### Q: What is the best way to rid my lawn of creeping sorrel?
A: The areas of the lawn where the infestation occurs can be sprayed with weedkiller like Turfweeder or Hormoban. Repeat after three to four weeks. It is also a good idea to apply Dolomitic Agricultural Lime at a rate of 180 g/m² to the lawn area infested with creeping sorrel. Water well after application. When fertilising the lawn with nitrogen, rather use a fertiliser like Wonder Lawns & Foliage 7:1:3 (21) + 27,6% Lime, where the added lime can help to prevent the soil from getting too acid. Sorrel prefers acid soil.

### Q: What is the best method for controlling dandelions?
A: They can be removed by hand as soon as they appear. Or spot-treat them with a sponge tied onto a little stick and dipped in a solution of Banweed M.C.P.A. Occasional plants can be controlled by cutting the tap root well below the soil level. It is interesting to note that dandelion (*Taraxacum officinale*) has been an important herbal medicine and food plant since the 13th century. Fresh leaves can be eaten raw in salads or added to stews and soups. The whole plant is rich in potassium, iron and magnesium plus vitamins A, B, C and D. It is used to treat constipation, gallstones, liver ailments, colds, coughs and chronic toxic ailments.

### Q: Every summer my garden gets invaded by purslane. What can I do?
A: Purslane (*Portulaca oleracea*), also known as pigweed, is an annual weed which grows fast in warm weather and rich soil. It has to be controlled by shallow cultivation when still small. Larger plants are difficult to

Pampas grass (*Cortaderia selloana*) has abrasive foliage and is highly invasive.

control in this way, as broken-off pieces will root and grow again. Control with weedkillers like Hormoban or Turfweeder. Purslane is also one of the ancient medicinal herbs, dating back over 2 000 years. It is rich in calcium and has natural antibiotic properties.

**Q: How can I get rid of morning glory without killing the rest of my garden plants?**
A: Morning glory (*Ipomoea purpurea*) is a fast-growing climber and very difficult to eradicate. The best way to go about controlling these plants is to destroy their root systems and remove all growth close to the ground. The rest will wilt and die and can be removed when dry.

**Q: How can I eradicate small guava trees? I regularly cut them off as low as possible, just to find them growing very well again after a few weeks.**
A: The best way to get rid of unwanted tree saplings is to apply the weedkiller Garlon 4 either to the foliage or painted onto the stems of unwanted plants. Use 20 ml Garlon, mixed with 1 litre diesel, for painting onto stems.

**Q: I am confused about which lantana plants to grow, as I have noticed many nurseries selling these plants. Is it not a declared noxious weed?**
A: *Lantana camara* is a very invasive plant and it is against the law to grow these anywhere in South Africa. It is possible that the invasive species has been confused with the noninvasive *Lantana montevidensis*, previously known as *Lantana sellowiana*, which is a lovely garden plant. There are currently five different varieties of *Lantana montevidensis* available at nurseries. These are grown as water-wise, ground-cover plants or small shrubs in full sun or partial shade. The different varieties are: *Lantana montevidensis* (purple lantana) with dull-green foliage and purple flowers almost throughout the year. *L. montevidensis* 'Malan's Gold' is low-growing with golden-yellow and green foliage. It grows in full sun and bears purple flowers from spring to summer. *L. montevidensis* 'Rosie' has dark-green foliage and bears pale-pink flowers in summer. *L. montevidensis* 'Sundancer' is a compact grower with bright-yellow flowers throughout the year. *L. montevidensis* 'White Lightning' is similar to the purple lantana, but bears white flowers on and off during the year.

**Q: What is the best way to get rid of weeds without using chemicals?**
A: The best method is the traditional way of digging, hoeing and hand-weeding. When digging an infested bed, try to remove every piece of root or bulb that is visible. Leave the bed fallow for as long as possible so that all newly sprouting weeds can be removed effectively by hoeing or hand-weeding. Regular hoeing of weeds before they have had time to seed themselves will clear the bed eventually. Another method is to smother weeds by covering them with black plastic sheeting to deprive them of light.

Bugtree (*Solanum mauritianum*) is a noxious weed introduced from South America.

# pests and diseases

Almost all gardens have plants that become spotted, yellowed or mottled in the foliage, distorted, scaly or stunted in growth. These are just a few easily recognised symptoms of plant disease. Plants may become ill due to various causes, apart from the fact that they might have been attacked by some organism, whether a fungus or an insect pest.

The climate and weather conditions, which affect growth, play a very important role in plant health. It is important to grow plants in their correct environment. Do not try to grow a tropical plant in an area that experiences frost during winter, for example. Pests and diseases can also attack plants grown under optimum conditions. It is a fact, however, that plants that grow under stressful conditions are more susceptible to attack by pests and diseases.

## Control of pests and diseases

This can be divided into physical, biological and chemical control. Physical control can be applied in some cases by removing aphids with a jet of water, for example, or washing off certain insects with soapy water. One can also physically catch and destroy certain insect pests without having to resort to chemical control.

Biological control can be obtained by introducing certain predator species for the control of specific insect pests; ladybirds, for example, prey on aphids. (See pages 29-31.)

Chemical control is the application of pesticides, which usually are poisonous substances, for the control of specific pests and diseases. Chemicals should always be used with discretion and in ways that will least affect beneficial insects and birds in the garden.

Pesticides are divided into insecticides and fungicides and were developed to help farmers and gardeners protect their crops and plants against pests and diseases. It is very important to identify the pest or disease correctly before applying any pesticide. If in doubt, take an example of the diseased plant to a reputable garden centre for expert advice on the correct control method. Pesticides must always be applied according to instructions on the label or enclosed pamphlet. Application quantities have been accurately determined through research and should never be changed. Pesticides must be used responsibly and with care, as these products usually are poisonous and can affect all living creatures.

Generally, two types of pesticides can be used, namely systemic and contact pesticides. Systemic pesticides are absorbed by the plant through its leaves and roots and translocated throughout the plant, so that the plant will be poisonous to the attacking organisms. Contact pesticides are those that should be applied to obtain total coverage. These pesticides are only effective if organisms come into direct contact with the pesticide. It is advisable to add a wetting agent like G-49 to help contact pesticides stick to foliage and obtain an even spread all over the plant.

The astylus beetle, feeding on pollen.

# Plant diseases

Diseases can be divided into parasitic and nonparasitic diseases. Parasitic diseases are caused by plant pathogens like fungi, bacteria and viruses and can attack any part of the plant. Examples of parasitic diseases are rusts, blights, mildews and moulds. Virus disease is recognised by mosaic or mottled patterns on foliage and can also cause stunted and distorted growth.

Nonparasitic diseases are physiological problems caused by nutrient deficiencies in the soil, chemical injuries caused by incorrect fertilisation, careless use of herbicides and adverse weather and growing conditions like inadequate watering and overwatering, sudden temperature changes, frost, windburn or hail damage, to name a few.

## Parasitic diseases

### Fungi

Fungus disease is the cause of most plant diseases and may be carried on the seeds, in the soil or on other plants and weeds by means of microscopic spores. Fungus spores can spread quickly through wind and water, especially during warm and humid weather. Fungus diseases can be grouped into four main groups according to the different disease symptoms they cause: leaf spots, rusts, mildews, stem and root rots.

**Leaf spots and blights.** These usually appear on foliage during spells of wet weather, but many can also appear during any weather conditions. Examples of these diseases are black spot on roses, dollar spot on lawns, anthracnose in pawpaws and mangoes, early and late blight on irises and vegetables like potatoes, tomatoes, carrots, parsnips and beets. These diseases can be prevented by means of one of the following sprays: Bravo 500, Coppercount-N, Dithane, Folicur, Funginex, Rosecare, Viricop, Rose and Garden Dust and Fungi Gun Aerosol. It is a good idea to alternate one or two products during the season to prevent the fungus building up resistance against a single fungicide.

**Rust.** The orange- or red-coloured pustules on leaves and stems, which break open and release a mass of spores, can easily identify rust fungus. The appearance of rust is usually dependent on weather conditions. It is a common disease on roses, calendulas, geraniums, gerberas and beans and can be reasonably controlled by weekly applications of copper-based fungicides (see under Leaf spots and blights).

**Mildew.** Powdery mildew is a fungus that appears as a whitish-grey powder on the surface of leaves. It may also occur on flowers and stems. Powdery mildew occurs most commonly on roses, dahlias, zinnias, calendulas, sweet peas and vine crops. This disease can be controlled by applications of sulphur or systemic fungicide like Bayleton A, Fungi Gun, Funginex, Rosecare and Rose and Garden Dust. Downy mildew is less common and usually occurs on the underside of new foliage as a greyish, velvet-like fungus. It may attack crops like grapes, vine crops, cabbages, onions, lettuce and plants like stocks during periods of wet weather. Spraying at ten-day intervals with a copper spray can control downy mildew. For roses, use Bayleton A, Fungi Gun, Funginex, Rosecare and Rose and Garden Dust.

**Stem and root rot.** The most common of these is damping-off disease of seeds and seedlings, caused by a soil-borne fungus active under damp conditions. To prevent seedlings from falling over at soil level, drench the soil with Fongarid or a copper-based mixture. Or sterilise the soil in seedling trays by baking the soil in the oven for 10 minutes at 60 °C. Root rot occurs in poorly drained soils under damp conditions on delphiniums, carnations, gerberas, strawberries and cabbages. Fruit trees like avocados and shrubs may also be attacked. The best method of control is to practise crop rotation and drench the soil with mixtures like Fongarid and Virikop.

## Bacteria

Bacterial disease is caused by bacteria, which are microscopic organisms with the ability to multiply very quickly. Bacteria are responsible for very serious diseases like bacterial spots, bacterial rots, bacterial wilt, crown gall and bacterial canker on crops like roses, tomatoes, potatoes, bulbs and corms, and fruit trees. Bacterial disease is fortunately not very common in the home garden, as no chemicals are available to control this disease effectively.

## Virus

Virus disease is also quite a serious disease and often occurs in the home garden. Viruses cause different symptoms in different plants. On the foliage they may cause mosaic, mottling, concentric rings or patterns, stripes or brown die-back. Foliage can also be curled, distorted or twisted. Flowers may have mottled petals, while other plants may be stunted and some may even die. There are no chemicals available that will control virus disease; the only way to prevent this disease from spreading is through practising hygiene. Virus disease can be passed on from diseased plants to healthy plants through pruning secateurs, handling and insects like aphids, thrips, whiteflies and grasshoppers. All plants suspected of virus disease have to be pulled out and destroyed by burning.

## Nonparasitic diseases

These are usually not real diseases but physiological disorders caused by factors like environment, climate, atmosphere, chemical damage, planting material and cultivation methods which influence the growth of plants. The environment in which plants grow plays a vital role in their health, for example indoor plants, which need a certain amount of light, water, humidity and a certain temperature to be healthy. If one of these factors is excessive or insufficient for the particular plant species it will develop symptoms like leaf drop, or the tips of the foliage may turn brown. Climate, wind, drought, rain, frost and hail may cause certain symptoms, which in their turn can cause secondary fungal infections. Atmosphere, salt-laden winds, dust, factory pollution and smog can all adversely affect healthy plant growth. Some plants are more resistant to these factors than others.

Chemical damage usually occurs with incorrect spray applications, where the strength of the spray may be too strong and cause leaf burn, for instance. Planting material, for example poor-quality seeds and propagation material, can result in weak plants.

Cultivation methods, the soil type and nutrient value greatly influence plant growth. Too much or too little of a certain mineral element can cause toxicity or deficiency symptoms. Drainage and the pH of the soil can also affect certain plant species more than others which are adapted to such conditions.

# Garden pests

Pests are insects and other creatures like beetles, bugs, caterpillars, aphids, mites, snails and slugs that do damage to plants by feeding on the foliage, roots or stem of the plant. Pests can be divided into two groups according to the way they feed: chewing insects and sap-sucking insects.

## Chewing insects

These are insects that eat the actual plant tissues – leaves, flowers, buds, stems or fruits. They include beetles, caterpillars, cutworm, grasshoppers, fruit fly and codling moth. Snails and slugs are not insects but are also included in this group. Chewing insects are controlled by contact or stomach poisons.

*Beetles*

**Astylus beetle.** A medium-sized, yellow beetle with black spots, which feeds on pollen during summer. Can be controlled with insecticides like Baysol Insecticide RTU, Bexadust, Everdeath, Malasol, Malathion, No Insect Outdoors and Rose and Garden Dust.

**Chafer beetle.** A medium-sized, shiny, coppery-brown beetle active during the night. Feeds on young flowers and shoots. Can be controlled with Bexadust, Everdeath, Folithion, Karbadust, Karbaspray, Stinkpowder and No Insect Outdoors RTU.

**CMR beetle.** A large beetle with black and yellow bands over the wings. Feeds mainly on flower petals. Can be controlled with Bexadust, Folithion, Malasol, Malathion and Rose and Garden Dust.

**Flower beetle.** A big, black-and-yellow beetle which feeds on ripe fruit and rose petals during summer. Can be controlled with Garden Ripcord and Folithion.

*Caterpillars*

Caterpillars, of which there are many different types, are the larval stage of butterflies and moths, which lay their eggs on leaves, flowers and fruit. When these eggs hatch the larvae feed on the leaves and fruit or flowers.

**American bollworm.** A brownish-black to green caterpillar with a lighter stripe along its sides. Feeds on buds, fruits and leaves. Can be controlled with Baysol, Chlorpirifos, Dursban 2E, Folithion, Garden Gun, Garden Ripcord, Natural Insecticide and No Insect Outdoors.

**Codling moth larvae.** These are pinkish with a darker head. They live by boring in fruit, causing rotten patches. Can be controlled with Garden Ripcord and Lebaycid. Start spraying when flowering is nearly over.

**Cutworm.** Greyish-brown, live underground and feed on stems of young plants just below the soil surface. Can be controlled with Chlorpirifos, Dursban 2E, Cutworm bait, Garden Ripcord.

**False codling moth larvae.** Light pink with a dark head and bore into fruit, causing rotten patches. Can be controlled with Garden Ripcord, Karbasol and Lebaycid.

**Fruit fly.** Brightly coloured, medium-sized flies which lay their eggs in fruit. When eggs hatch, white maggots infest fruit. Can be controlled with Garden Ripcord, Lebaycid, Malasol + Sugar (bait treatment).

**Lawn caterpillars.** These are greenish-brown and are active during the night. They hide just below the soil surface during the day. Can be controlled with Bexadust, Chlorpirifos, Dursban 2E, Dipterex, Everdeath, Garden Ripcord, Karbadust, Karbaspray, Malasol, Malathion, 4:1:1 (21) + Karbaspray and Stinkpowder.

**Lily borer caterpillars.** These have yellow and black bands around the body. Young caterpillars feed by boring into lily leaves and moving down into the bulb. They appear during the summer months. Can be controlled with Garden Ripcord.

*Grasshoppers*

Many different species, from small to large, can be found in gardens. They feed on foliage and are usually only a pest in gardens that are close to the open veld. They can be controlled with Bexadust, Folithion, Malasol, Karbadust, Karbaspray and Stinkpowder.

*Crickets*

They are dark grey to black and can be small to large. They usually feed on lawn grasses, strawberries and vegetables and can be controlled with Bexadust, Karbadust, Everdeath, Chlorpirifos, Dursban 2E, Garden Ripcord and Folithion.

Mole crickets (Parktown prawns) are large, coppery-brown crickets with long forelegs. They are usually active in damp weather on summer nights. They can be controlled with a solution of Garden Ripcord or Folithion. Pour 50 ml of the mixture down each hole.

### Ants

Many different species occur in home gardens, especially in lawns and flowerbeds. They can be controlled with Chlorpirifos, Dursban 2E, Garden Ripcord, Folithion, Malasol, Ant Dust, Everdeath and Stinkpowder.

Harvester termites are white or light brown, live in underground colonies and can be a problem in lawns. They can be controlled with Baythion Ant, Garden Ripcord, Kamikaze, Termite Bait and Zero Harvester.

### Snails and slugs

These pests are usually active at night during wet weather. They eat flower petals and foliage. They can be controlled with Mesurol, Sluggem, Snailban and Snailflo.

## Sap-sucking insects

These insects live by sucking sap from plant tissues and can reduce the vitality of the plant seriously. They can also carry virus disease from one plant to another. Sap suckers include insects like aphids, Australian bug, cochineal, mealybug, psylla, pumpkin fly, red spider mite, scale, stinkbug, thrips and whitefly. Systemic and contact insecticides can control these insects.

### Aphids

Also known as greenfly, these are small, soft-bodied, green to black insects usually found on new shoots and flower buds. They can be controlled with contact and stomach formulations like Chlorpirifos, Dursban 2E, Garden Ripcord, Folithion, Malasol, Malathion, Rosecare; ready-to-use formulations like Baysol, Everdeath, Garden Gun, No Insect Outdoors RTU, Pirimor and Rose and Garden Dust; systemic formulations like Aphicide, Insecticide Granules and Metasystox R; and natural organic formulations like Natural Insecticide and Naturen Rape Oil Insecticide.

### Australian bug

This is a soft, scaly insect with a large egg sac covered in white wax. Usually found on new shoots and under leaves. Can be controlled with Baysol Insecticide RTU, Garden Gun, Malasol, Malathion, No Insect Outdoors RTU and Oleum.

### Mealybug

These are small, oval, pink-coloured insects covered in white, waxy threads, usually found on tender new growth. Can be controlled with Aphicide, Baysol, Chlorpirifos, Dursban 2E, Garden Gun, Garden Ripcord, Malasol, Malathion, Natural Insecticide, No Insect Outdoors RTU and Rose and Garden Dust.

The mole cricket (top); chafer beetle (middle); and flower beetle (bottom).

Black spot on rose leaves (top); leaves showing signs of virus disease (middle); and powdery mildew (bottom).

*Psylla*

Small insects not easily seen. Their presence is seen by damage to leaves, which results in bumps on the surface of leaves. Especially noted on citrus leaves. Plants will not die of psylla attack. They can be controlled with Aphicide, Chlorpirifos, Dursban 2E and Metasystox R.

*Red spider mite*

These are very small, dark-red, eight-legged mites usually found on the undersides of leaves. They sometimes produce a fine, white web and cause leaves to have small, yellow dots on the surface, turning to a silver-grey colour which later turns brown before leaves drop. Can be controlled with Chlorpirifos, Dursban 2E, Garden Gun, Oleum, Naturen Rape Oil Insecticide, Redspidercide, Redspiderspray, Spidermitespray and Stinkpowder.

*Scale*

Many different varieties occur in gardens. They are usually round or pear-shaped and grey, reddish-brown, brown or purple in colour. They attach themselves to bark, stems and leaves. Scale can be controlled with Chlorpirifos, Dursban 2E, Folithion, Garden Gun, Malasol, Malathion and Oleum.

*Whitefly*

A small, white-winged fly found on the undersides of leaves, especially those of fuchsias. They can be controlled with Garden Gun, Garden Ripcord, Natural Insecticide, No Insect Outdoors RTU and Whitefly Insecticide.

## Questions and answers

**Q: My palm leaves are covered in a black, soot-like layer. How can I get rid of this problem?**

A: The black, soot-like layer is called sooty mould and is a fungus that lives on honeydew, excreted by scale insects and aphids. You will probably also notice ants on your palm, as they feed on honeydew and, to enable them to obtain more, they carry the young insects to other parts of the plant to start new colonies. You will have to kill the ants and the scale insects. The sooty mould will stop growing as soon as the honeydew dries up. You can rinse the leaves with soapy water (5 ml dishwashing liquid in 1 litre of water) to wash off the sooty mould.

**Q: My peach trees have gum oozing through the bark. The trees look sad and leaves are starting to drop.**

A: Your trees are suffering from gummosis, which is caused by a fungus present in soils. In wet conditions roots start to weaken and the fungus then attacks the plant. You can treat the soil by drenching the root zone with a copper-based fungicide like Virikop. The stem and branches must also be sprayed with copper spray in autumn and spring. Make sure that all surfaces are covered well.

**Q: My lemon tree is suffering from malformed, crinkly and bunched-up leaves covered in little lumps.**

A: Your lemon tree is suffering an attack from citrus psylla, which is a small insect that sucks sap on the undersides of leaves and causes bumps to form on the upper leaf surface. Heavy infestations can cause leaves to turn yellow and fall off. Treat with Aphicide as a soil application at the start of a new growth flush, or spray with Metasystox R. Do not harvest any lemons from treated trees for at least eight weeks.

**Q: My tomatoes, carrots, beetroot and lettuce all develop swollen nodules on the roots, and the plants are stunted and no longer bear well.**

A: Your vegetable garden is infested by nematodes or eelworm. It is a very small worm that invades roots, causing them to swell up and form nodules which disturb the flow of sap, causing the plant to become stunted and wilted. You have to dig up plants carefully, with as many roots as possible, and burn them. Plant marigolds or 'kakiebos' weed in your vegetable garden and dig it in as a green manure crop as soon as the first flowers start to open. You can also starve the nematodes by keeping the soil fallow for two years and removing every weed and plant as soon as it appears. The soil and crops can also be treated with pesticides like Basamid and Nemacur respectively.

**Q: My compost area is infested by hundreds of earwigs. How can I get rid of this pest?**

A: There is a traditional method of catching earwigs. Fill an empty flowerpot with newspaper or straw and set it, inverted, on a cane on the compost heap. Earwigs are active during the night and will retire to the pot to sleep away the day. It is easy to destroy the contents of the pot and to set it up again. The problem will be reduced considerably after a few days. You can also deal with them by spraying the area with Natural Insecticide. Turn the compost over to cover as much material as possible. Repeat when necessary. You can also use Bexadust or Karbadust.

**Q: What exactly is lime sulphur?**

A: The active ingredient is polysulphide sulphur. It is a fungicide and often acts as an insecticide as well. It is very effective to use as a dormant spray, after pruning, to control fungus, scale insects and mites on plants like roses, peaches and other deciduous fruit trees. It does not keep for a long time and needs to be used as fresh as possible. It is quite safe to use in the garden as it has very low toxicity levels. Follow application rates carefully, as new growth can easily burn if sprayed with the winter strength.

**Q: Can I use more than one pesticide, mixed together, to make up a spray cocktail?**

A: It is not advisable to mix pesticides together, as different pesticides can react with each other and negatively influence the effectiveness of the spray. Organisms can also build up a resistance to certain pesticides, and if a cocktail is used it will be difficult to determine to which active ingredient an organism has built up resistance. There are, however, certain pesticides that can be safely mixed without adverse effects. Consult the enclosed information pamphlets carefully before making up cocktails.

**Q: What is the best way to treat stem borer on my rose bushes?**

A: The borer is actually a carpenter bee, which is a useful predator in the garden as it catches other insects to put in the stems for the young to feed on when they hatch. You could use a Karbaspray paste to smear on cut surfaces immediately after cutting, or plug up holes to prevent water entering the stems, which helps prevent the stems from dying back.

# regional gardening problems

Gardening is a very popular pastime in our warm climate, because gardens are used as extensions of the home. There are about five major climatic zones in South Africa, each characterised by its own unique climatic conditions. Exceptions do occur, such as isolated frost pockets in some zones, and micro-climatic conditions within gardens make it possible to grow plants from different climatic regions. It makes sense, however, to try to copy nature by growing plants indigenous to your region, as these plants thrive in your particular area and will need less feeding and watering to look good throughout the year. It is important to have a good selection of indigenous and exotics, as it is not always practical to grow only indigenous plants because of microclimate differences and personal tastes and preferences.

Soils differ widely throughout the different climatic zones. In some parts soils are naturally rich in nutrients and organic material, but these are very few and far between. Most soils need to be enriched with organic matter and fertilisers, as the leaching effect of the sun and rain in shallow topsoil makes it impossible to maintain a healthy soil structure. Heavy clay soils need coarse river sand to facilitate better drainage, and very sandy soils need lots of organic material to help with moisture retention. See pages 21-25 for more information on soils and fertilisers.

Indigenous plants have become very popular in recent years, partly because of severe droughts that frequently occur in parts of the country, but also because these plants attract wildlife to the garden. Another reason for their popularity is that many outstanding varieties, including new hybrids, have become available. The botanical gardens have been very helpful in supplying and promoting indigenous plants. These days many nurseries fortunately have an indigenous section to help make these plants available.

## Climatic zones

### 1. Coastal summer rainfall and subtropical regions

The region is characterised by dry, frost-free winters. It includes the eastern parts of Mpumalanga and the coastal parts of KwaZulu-Natal and the Eastern Cape as far south as Port Elizabeth. The southern part of this region experiences winter rainfall and strong winds. The rainfall of the rest of the region ranges between 700 mm

Indigenous crocosmias, commonly known as montbretias, grow well in temperate regions.

and 1 500 mm, resulting in high humidity during summer. Light frost can occur in isolated pockets. Soils are viable and fertile, ranging from loam to sandy loam. Plants in this region grow rapidly because of the high rainfall and hot temperatures and require regular attention, such as pruning and weeding. Subtropical plants and palms thrive in this region. Close to the coast, choose plants that are flexible, like restios, grasses and reeds, and shrubs with thick, glossy leaves like the Indian hawthorn (*Raphiolepis indica*), for example. Many grey- and hairy-leaved plants are well adapted for dry and windy areas, including salt-laden air at the coast.

Strong wind along the coast is part of the climate, and one has to adapt to it by providing plants with shelter from the wind and planting species that can cope with these conditions. The effect of wind on the coast differs from place to place, and in very exposed areas winds can cause severe damage to plants.

A coastal windbreak is essential to provide shelter and to create a microclimate for more tender plants. It is a good idea to start planting lower-growing, wind-hardy plants facing the sea, with taller plants behind them. Always use coarse mulch around plants to conserve moisture, to keep the roots cool and to help with weed control.

The following are proven, tough, lower-growing plants to consider: *Carissa macrocarpa* (Natal plum or amatungulu), *Chrysanthemoides monilifera* (bush-tick berry), *Coprosma repens* (mirror plant), *Helichrysum cymosum*, *Rhagodia hastata* (salt bush), *Rhus crenata* (dune crowberry), *Salvia africana-lutea* (beach salvia).

Taller plants to establish behind these lower plants are: *Aloe* spp., *Buddleja salviifolia* (sagewood), *Callistemon* spp. (bottlebrush), *Dodonaea angustifolia* (sand olive), *Dodonaea angustifolia* 'Atropurpurea' (purple hop bush ), *Mimusops caffra* (coastal red milkwood), *Phylica buxifolia* (box hard-leaf), *Portulacaria afra* (spekboom), *Plumbago auriculata* (blue plumbago), *Tecomaria capensis* (Cape honeysuckle), *Westringia fruticosa* (Australian rosemary).

Wind-hardy trees to consider as windbreaks and tall hedges: *Brachylaena discolor* subsp. *discolor* (coast silver oak), *Lagunaria patersonii* (pyramid tree), *Mimusops caffra* (coastal red milkwood), *Myoporum insulare* (manatoka), *Phoenix canariensis* (Canary Island date palm), *Phoenix reclinata* (wild date palm), *Sideroxylon inerme* (white milkwood), *Tarchonanthus camphoratus* (wild camphor bush).

Windbreaks like walls and fences can be erected, but be sure to provide holes in the construction to filter the wind. Solid walls will only channel the force of the wind and create turbulence.

Separate windbreaks around single plants can also be constructed, especially where larger specimens are planted. Always stake plants well and build a half-shield with shade cloth, wood, reeds or hessian on the wind side to shelter the plant until well established.

## 2. Coastal winter rainfall region

The southwestern Cape is a virtually frost-free region with cool days in winter, where subtropical plants do well in warm, sheltered and well-watered positions. Close to the coast the wind is strong, with southeasterly winds in summer and gale-force northwesterly winter storms.

Rainfall in this region ranges between 300 and 2 000 mm. The mountainous parts experience colder winters with occasional frost and snow. Soils are mainly sandy and acidic with deep, alkaline sands in some areas close to the coast. Buffalo quick-grass (*Stenotaphrum secundatum*) makes the best lawn in this region. Proteas, restios and fynbos species thrive here.

The same measures against wind as for the previous region can be applied here, and the wind-hardy plants listed above can also be used in this region.

High alkalinity in most coastal, sandy soils makes them unsuitable for many plants that prefer acid soil. Hydrangeas usually bear pink flowers in these areas, which is a sure sign of alkaline soil. Phosphate and some

Drought-resistant *Tulbaghia violacea*, commonly known as wild garlic.

micronutrients like iron and aluminium become unavailable in these soils, causing deficiency symptoms, poor flower formation and stunted growth on plants like azaleas, camellias, gardenias, fuchsias, tea bushes and magnolias. The best way to overcome this problem is to grow plants that can tolerate alkaline soil. A good indication of which plants to grow would be to stick to indigenous flora from the region. Always add lots of compost and superphosphate to holes and beds when planting, and keep plants mulched at all times. Once plants are well established the garden can be fertilised three times a year with ammonium sulphate (alum) or flowers of sulphur at recommended rates to lower the soil pH. Plants showing deficiency symptoms can be treated with trace element solutions like Trelmix or Iron Chelate. Where brak borehole water is a problem, gypsum (calcium sulphate) can be used by either sprinkling it around plants or treating the reservoir water before watering.

Some shrubs that tolerate alkaline conditions are: *Argyranthemum* spp. (daisy bushes), \**Barleria obtusa* (bush violet), \**Burchellia bubalina* (wild pomegranate), *Ceratostigma willmottianum* (Chinese plumbago), \**Coleonema* spp. (confetti bush), *Echium fastuosum* (pride of Madeira), *Escallonia* spp., \**Euryops* spp., *Grevillea* spp., *Lantana montevidensis*, *Lavandula* spp. (lavender), *Nerium oleander* (oleander), \**Plectranthus* spp., \**Plumbago auriculata* (blue plumbago), \**Polygala myrtifolia* (September bush or wild violet), *Rosmarinus officinalis* (rosemary), \**Tecomaria capensis* (Cape honeysuckle).

Perennials that tolerate alkaline soil are: \**Agapanthus* spp., \**Clivia miniata* (bush lily), *Dianthus* spp. (carnations), \**Felicia amelloides* (blue marguerite), \**Gazania* spp., *Hemerocallis* spp. (day lilies), *Limonium perezii* (statice), \**Osteospermum* spp., \**Pelargonium* spp.

## 3. Winter rainfall dry continental region

This is the Karoo and Namaqualand west coast region that experiences winter rainfall. The eastern parts of this region may experience some summer rainfall occasionally. Light frost may occur with heavier frost on the inland mountainous regions. Rainfall ranges between 25 and 350 mm. Soils are mainly sandy loam, rich in minerals.

Subtropical plants will thrive in sheltered and well-watered areas. Succulents and drought-tolerant indigenous plants thrive in this region. Install rainwater tanks to catch all runoff water from the roof. Keep the level of organic matter, in and on the soil surface, high to help with water retention. Consider a drip irrigation system for watering shrubs and trees. Use containers to grow succulents and group them together around the house.

Some trees that would do well in this region are: *Acacia erioloba* (camel thorn), *Casuarina stricta*, *Ceratonia siliqua* (carob), *Eucalyptus cinerea* (florist's gum), *Olea europaea* subsp. *africana* (wild olive), *Phoenix canariensis* (Canary Island date palm), *Phoenix dactylifera* (date palm), *Populus deltoides* (cottonwood), *Rhus lancea* (karree), *Schinus molle* (pepper tree), *Washingtonia filifera* (petticoat palm).

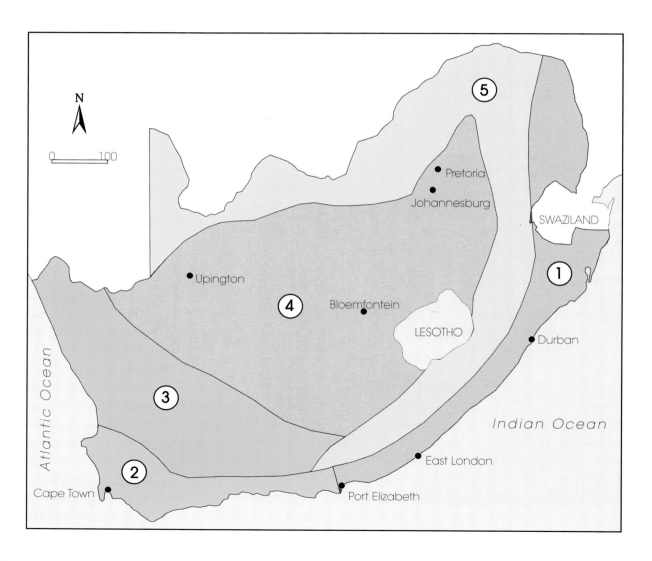

## 4. Summer rainfall dry continental and highveld region

This is the dry inland region and comprises the Karoo, Free State and northern highveld regions of the country. Rainfall is mainly in summer, with dry winters and severe frost.

Rainfall varies between 75 mm in the west and 1 000 mm in the east. The soil in this region is mainly sandy loam to clay loam and fertile. Install an automatically controlled irrigation system for more efficient irrigation and better water conservation. Always group plants with similar water requirements together in the same bed. Plant living mulches to reduce water evaporation, prevent weed problems and keep soil temperatures down. Only frost-resistant plants should be considered for this region.

Some excellent frost-hardy shrubs with good colour, shape and texture for this region are: *Abelia grandiflora* 'Francis Mason', *Aloysia triphylla* (lemon verbena), azaleas, *Berberis* varieties, *Buddleja* spp. (butterfly bush), *Camellia sasanqua*, conifers, *Cotoneaster apiculatus* (*C. horizontalis*), *Deutzia scabra* 'Flora Plena' (bridal wreath), *Escallonia* spp., *Euonymus japonicus* varieties, *Hydrangea quercifolia* (oak-leaf hydrangea), *Ilex aquifolium* (common holly), *Ilex cornuta* 'Burfordii' (Burford's holly), *Laurus nobilis* (bay laurel), *Lavandula* spp. (lavender), *Leonotis leonurus* var. *leonurus* (wild dagga), *Ligustrum lucidum* 'Tricolor' (Chinese privet), *Ligustrum ovalifolium* 'Aureum' (golden privet), magnolia varieties, *Melianthus major* (honey bush), *Myrtus communis* (common myrtle), *Nandina domestica* varieties (sacred bamboo), *Photinia x fraseri* 'Red Robin', *Prunus laurocerasus* (English laurel), *Raphiolepis x delacourii* 'Kruschenii', roses, *Sarcococca confusa* (Christmas box), *Spiraea thunbergii* (baby may), *Viburnum macrocephalum* 'Sterile' (Chinese snowball).

## 5. Summer rainfall bushveld region

This is the northern part of the country. It is characterised by hot summers and dry, mild winters with isolated frost in high-lying areas. The eastern part receives about 800 mm rain per annum, and the northern and western regions only about 400 mm in summer. The soils range from sandy loam to clay loam and are fertile. High summer temperatures must be taken into consideration when planting new plants; extra maintenance in pruning may be necessary due to some plants that grow very fast. Most plants, except tropical plants, and especially indigenous trees and shrubs, do well in this region. This is the ideal region for creating a woodland garden. Groups of trees will provide a shady canopy for shade-tolerant plants and filter cool air through your garden during the hot summer months. Choose trees indigenous to your area, as they will be best acclimatised to your region.

Some shade-tolerant plants for this region are: *Aspidistra elatior* (cast-iron plant), *Barleria repens*, *Carissa macrocarpa* 'Green Carpet' (dwarf Natal plum), *Clivia miniata* (bush lily), *Dietes grandiflora* (large wild iris), *Eucomis* spp. (pineapple flower), *Plectranthus* spp., *Ruscus aculeatus* (butcher's broom), *Sansevieria trifasciata* (mother-in-law's tongue), *Sansevieria hyacinthoides* (piles root), *Scadoxus puniceus* (dwarf paintbrush), *Scilla natalensis* (blue squill), *Tradescantia pallida* 'Purple Heart'.

## Questions and answers

**Q: We live on the coast and our soil is very alkaline. What can we do to grow acid-soil-loving plants?**
A: The best way to grow acid-loving plants in your garden would be to grow them in suitable pots with acid potting soil. These pots can be planted into the garden. Mulch each plant with acid compost such as composted pine bark, pine needles or peat moss. You can also, with some effort, prepare beds with acidic soil to grow acid-soil-loving plants, but this would be a temporary measure.

A group of sun-loving ground covers massed together.

**Q: We live on the Highveld. Which water-wise ground covers can we plant in full sun to act as living mulches?**

A: It is a good idea to use ground covers massed in large swathes rather than having many different varieties planted together. Always choose plants for the appropriate growing conditions – for example, sun-loving plants in full sun and shade lovers in shade, etc.

Some drought-tolerant ground covers are: *Aptenia cordifolia* (heart leaf), *Armeria maritima* (sea pink), *Bulbine frutescens* (stalked bulbine), *Carpobrotus edulis* (sour fig), *Cotyledon* spp., *Crassula* spp., *Dianthus deltoides* (pink), *Dymondia margaretae* (silver carpet), *Echeveria* spp., *Erigeron karvinskianus* (erigeron daisies), *gazanias, *Lampranthus* spp. (vygies), *Osteospermum* spp., *Othonna* spp., *Polygonum capitatum* (knotweed), *Rosmarinus officinalis* 'Prostratus' (creeping rosemary), *Sedum acre* (wallpepper), *Stachys byzantina* (lamb's ear), *Tulbaghia violacea* (purple wild garlic), verbena hybrids.

**Q: I would like to grow vegetables during winter, but we experience heavy frost. How can I go about producing vegetables?**

A: Remember that plants suffering from water stress will suffer much more easily from frost scorch than well-watered plants. Always water your vegetable garden early in the day so that the soil is moist, with no surface water on the ground or foliage by nightfall. You will have to provide your vegetables with frost cover. One method is to use a floating frost cover, which consists of thin, white sheeting. This allows enough light and water through but does not prevent plants from suffering severe frost damage. However, it is a very good way of producing frost-tolerant vegetables like cabbages, lettuce and spinach, as it boosts growth and productivity considerably. Secure the sheeting with stones at the edges to prevent it from blowing away. It is also a very good way to protect vegetables against bird damage.

You can also put up a permanent structure and cover it with 30% shade cloth, which will have the benefit of being at least 2 to 3 °C warmer on frosty mornings. It also provides bird and hail protection.

Another option is to construct mini-tunnels over your vegetable beds by covering rounded frames, placed at 1-m intervals, with clear plastic sheeting of 50 microns or more. Cover the overlapping plastic on the sides with soil to prevent the wind from ripping it off.

## Q: Can you give me some advice on which colourful plants to grow in my holiday coastal garden?
A: Some interesting plants to consider would be: *Acalypha* hybrids (Jacob's coat), *Agave* spp., *Allamanda cathartica* (shrubby allamanda), *Arctotis* spp., *Bougainvillea* hybrids, *Codiaeum variegatum* (croton), *Dietes grandiflora* (large wild iris), *Euryops virgineus* (river resin bush), *Melaleuca bracteata* 'Johannesburg Gold' (golden melaleuca), *Pelargonium* spp., *Phormium tenax* (flax), *Raphiolepis x delacourii* 'Kruschenii', *Salvia chamelaeagnea* (light-blue sage), *Strelitzia reginae* (crane flower).

## Q: The soil in my garden in the Western Cape looks as if it has an oily layer and it does not absorb water well. What can I do to improve it?
A: The soil in your area is very sandy and is naturally very low in organic matter and clay. The soil does not really have an oily layer. The situation is caused by a high concentration of dead bacteria in the topsoil layer. These dead bacteria fill the spaces between sand particles and cause a water-repellent action. To improve the soil you will have to enlarge the pore space of the soil to facilitate easier water penetration. Do this by digging in lots of coarse compost and organic matter. You can also mix moisture-retaining ingredients into the soil like Terrasorb or Saturaid. Keep the soil well mulched at all times with coarse organic material.

## Q: Our soil seems to be pure sand on the KwaZulu-Natal north coast. In what quantities should compost and manure be added to encourage healthy plant growth?
A: To improve the soil, you will have to add about a barrowload of compost per square metre plus a light sprinkling of bone meal. Old, well-rotted manure can be added at about half a barrowload per square metre. Always keep the surface of the soil well mulched. By doing this you will eventually build up the organic matter in the top layer of the soil.

## Q: How can we utilise water more efficiently in the garden?
A: You can reduce the surface area of your lawn and create gravel pathways through tough, drought-tolerant plants, or enlarge beds with lots of organic mulch or water-wise ground covers. Choose the right lawn grass for your area. Raise the edges of garden beds and make shallow basins around trees and shrubs to prevent runoff. Add lots of compost to soil to help with water retention when preparing beds. Always use mulch to reduce evaporation and runoff. Group plants together according to their water requirements to make watering easier. Use an automatic irrigation system for more efficient watering. Use a drip irrigation system for trees and shrubs to reduce evaporation. During summer, irrigate during the night when temperatures and evaporation rates are lower. Install a rainwater tank to collect rainwater from the roof. Do not water on windy days and only start to water when plants are starting to wilt. Always water slowly so that water can penetrate to a good depth, which will encourage plants to develop a deep root system. Shallow watering will only encourage roots to develop close to the surface and plants will need much more water, as the topsoil dries out much faster than deeper down. Make sure that taps and irrigation systems are not leaking.

# references

Allan, Harriet B. 1993. *Palmers Garden Show Guide to Gardening in New Zealand.* Random House, Auckland.

Allen, Oliver E. 1984. *Pruning and Grafting.* Time-Life Books, Amsterdam.

Austin, David. 1997. *David Austin's English Roses.* Little Brown & Company, London.

Barnhoorn, F. 1995. *Growing Bulbs in South Africa.* Southern Book Publishers, Halfway House.

Beckett, K.A. 1987. *The RHS Encyclopaedia of House Plants.* Century, London.

Bird, Richard. 1996. *Gardeners' Questions Answered.* Salamander Books, London.

Brickell, C. 1990. *The Royal Horticultural Society Gardeners' Encyclopedia of Plants & Flowers.* Dorling Kindersley, London.

Brookes, John. 1998. *The New Garden.* Dorling Kindersley, London.

Dietz, Marjorie J. 1974 (ed.). *10,000 Garden Questions Answered by 20 Experts.* Doubleday & Company, New York.

Efekto. *Product Guide for the Home Garden.*

Gilbert, Zoë. 1983. *Gardening in South Africa.* Struik, Cape Town.

Henderson, L. & Musil, K.J. 1987. 'Plant Invaders of the Transvaal.' Bulletin 412. Department of Agriculture and Water Supply, Pretoria.

Heritage, Bill. 1976. *The Lotus Book of Water Gardening.* Hamlyn, London.

Hessayon, D.G. 1984. *The Flower Expert.* Pan Britannica Industries, Herts.

Hessayon, D.G. 1980. *The House Plant Expert.* Pan Britannica Industries, Herts.

Joffe, Pitta. 1993. *Die Tuinier se Gids tot Suid-Afrikaanse Plante.* Delos, Cape Town.

Kirsten, Keith. 1992. *Keith Kirsten's Complete Garden Manual for South Africa.* Human & Rousseau, Cape Town.

Köhlein, F. & Menzel, P. 1992. *Das neue grosse Blumenbuch. Stauden und Sommerblumen.* E.U. Verlag Eugen Ulmer, Germany.

Loxton, H. 1991. *The Garden.* Bok Books International, Durban.

Macoboy, Stirling. 1986. *Annuals for All Seasons.* Lansdowne Press, Sydney.

Midgley, K. 1991. *Garden Design.* Pelham Books, London.

Newman, Kenneth. 1991. *Newman's Garden Birds.* Southern Book Publishers, Halfway House.

Pienaar, Kristo. 1984. *The South African What Flower is That?* Struik, Cape Town.

Powrie, Fiona. 1998. *Grow South African Plants.* Kirstenbosch Gardening Series. National Botanical Institute, Cape Town.

Sheat, W.G. 1982. *The A to Z of Gardening in South Africa.* Struik, Cape Town.

Stirton, C.H. (ed.). 1978. *Plant Invaders: Beautiful, but Dangerous.* Department of Nature and Environmental Conservation of the Cape Provincial Administration, Cape Town.

Sunset Editions. 1981. *New Western Garden Book.* Lane Publishing Co., USA.

Swindells, Phillip. 1981. *Making the Most of Water Gardening.* Floraprint, Nottingham.

Trendler, R. & Hes, L. 1994. *Attracting Birds to your Garden in South Africa.* Struik, Cape Town.

Wager, V.A. 1984. *Plant Pests and Diseases: Prevention and Cure.* Jonathan Ball Publishers, Johannesburg.

*Yates Garden Guide*, Centennial Edition, 1895–1995. HarperCollins Publishers, Australia.

# Index